Everyday BBQ

All year outdoor grilling

Everyday BBQ
All year outdoor grilling

ANDREAS RUMMEL

GRUB STREET • LONDON

CONTENTS

DEAR FELLOW BARBECUERS...

I'm often asked whether I still like to barbecue at home. The answer is clear: of course I enjoy barbecuing in my private life. Everybody knows how good it feels to receive praise after a meal, and I'm no exception.

From March to October I'm almost always on a barbecuing mission – I sometimes actually feel like a missionary of the culinary sort, leading stray sheep onto the right path, never hesitating to take drastic measures in order to show others the road to pleasure. The rest of the time, I take to my barbecue at home, mostly for scientific purposes. That's when I try out the theories, cooking processes and foods that I've picked up, seen or researched over the course of the year. At certain times, mostly while driving between locations, I have flashes of inspiration, which I then put into practice. Part of this involves working with previously unfamiliar foods and ingredients. I then refine many of the 'experiments' until they are turned into new, creative recipes – often, too, so that I can explain myself clearly at my next seminar or in conversations with my peers. Some ideas – and their results – end up being tossed in the bin.

Some of my recipes are the direct results of problems I've encountered while barbecuing, such as the salmon fillet smoked over hot stones inside a side compartment accessory for the barbecue, which you will find on page 171. Others are simply the creative use of leftovers, such as the recipes using the waffle iron. I often know in advance whether something will work or not.

I rely on my intuition, and I naturally take advantage of my experience. The term food pairing refers to the art of combining ingredients. I have some books on the subject and my research regularly takes me to relevant Internet sites. I quite often come across sensational combinations.

For me, the most important thing is never to put the brakes on your creativity. You don't need to invite guests over as a reason to barbecue. You can't become a good pitmaster if you only bring out the barbecue two weeks every summer. Athletes have to train often and regularly if they want to be successful, hence my motto, 'learning by burning'.

To guide you along your journey to year-round barbecuing, this book contains recipes for both beginners and advanced barbecuers. You don't need to follow each recipe to the letter. Consider them also a stimulus for your own creativity. Since the knowledge I have built up over the years is only a fraction of what I still have left to learn about food and the possible ways of preparing it – not just on the barbecue – I remain inquisitive and open to everything. I hope you enjoy this book.

Andreas Rummel

There are as many types of barbecues as there are barbecuers. What they all have in common is the grill and the flame. Five-course meals, ribs for five hundred people, quesadillas for two, or a quick burger – everything is possible. **WHATEVER** food comes to mind, it's already been cooked by somebody on a barbecue. **WHEREVER** you are – in the mountains, by the sea, at a pool, in a car park or on a ship – somebody has already barbecued there. **HOW** or what you barbecue with – charcoal, briquettes, gas, electricity or a hot car bonnet – every heat source has been used before. **WHEN?** Any day is a good day for a barbecue!

Use your barbecue every day, whether in spring, summer, autumn or winter, hot or cold weather. Your barbecue is an extension of your kitchen. Barbecuing is a healthy, creative and versatile way to prepare extra delicious food. Andreas Rummel has compiled a range of varied recipes for you in this book. Whether simple or elaborate, there is something for you for every season. Try them out; they work! No matter if you use one of our Napoleon models or any other, you should start up your barbecue more often. The main thing is to do it!

We hope you will be trying out one of Andreas' recipes on your barbecue soon.

Happy barbecuing
Michael Voragen & Fred Schalkwijk
Napoleon Grills

GET
BARBECUING

BARBECUES, ACCESSORIES, TIPS AND TRICKS

WHY A GAS BARBECUE?

I'm a big fan of barbecuing with gas. I love the flexibility and immediateness that it offers compared to using charcoal. I can get home and quickly have delicious things laid out on the barbecue without having to heat up the grill and mess about with the charcoal. Moreover, I can have different sorts of foods cooking at the same time, and the zones of direct and indirect heat can be easily adjusted.

Since an experienced and versatile barbecuer lets the barbecue do most of the work, without needing to open the lid to check on the food, having a gas barbecue is a big advantage because the temperature can easily be adjusted between 80°C/176°F and 400°C/752°F. I choose the right temperature for the food and then take care of other things as it cooks.

The Triumph 410 pictured here is a space-saver with its folding side shelves. Its three burners and one side burner make it a culinary all-rounder.

ALWAYS CHOOSE THE RIGHT BARBECUE

With a portable gas barbecue, you can barbecue anytime and anywhere. There is enough room to cook practically an entire meal on one of these efficient and compact barbecues. Each burner has its own ignition and controls, allowing direct and indirect cooking, and with the Napoleon smoker tube, you can even turn your TravelQ™ into a smoker.

For year-round pleasure, **LEX** is a multi-purpose barbecue for style-conscious pitmasters. And the all-rounder among gas barbecues featuring infrared technology is the **LE3**, with its **SIZZLE ZONE**™ infrared side burner.

Triumph: the practical and high-quality Napoleon Triumph series scores highly with its space-saving design.

The **kettle barbecue** – here with lid and robust hinge – has become iconic. Some foods are only fun to cook over charcoal. The huge cast-iron grid guarantees good results, while creative use can be made of the chimney starter for cooking with a wok.

THE BEST EQUIPMENT AND ACCESSORIES

A smoking tube gives your food a light smoky flavour and turns slow-cooking cuts into a hearty smoked meal. Apple, cherry, hickory, maple and mesquite wood, and whisky oak barrel wood make good smoking chips.

Essential for the right grip: stainless steel barbecue tongs.

Barbecue tweezers for barbecuing and serving fragile food.

Knowing the internal temperature of the meat will finally put an end to the guess work – the barbecue meat lottery will be a thing of the past. A MUST for every barbecuing enthusiast who loves their meat perfectly cooked.

Digital wireless meat thermometer.

Probe thermometer for fast temperature checking in the meantime.

Spatula for turning over burgers, fish and other ingredients that could easily fall apart.

Double mini burger press

Burger presses, also suitable for preparing
stuffed burgers – the hot trend in America
right now.

Charcoal basket for applying
top heat manually (not
commercially available).

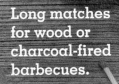

Heat-resistant gloves

Long matches
for wood or
charcoal-fired
barbecues.

Fish basket, suitable for three quite large fish, such as mackerel, Arctic char and trout. Remember to oil the metal before use!

Charcoal tray for gas barbecues – for those who can't do without charcoal.

Cast-iron griddle insert, for any fragile or small food that can fall through the grid – essential for versatile barbecuing. Great for making cooked breakfasts on the barbecue, such as pancakes, fried eggs, French toast and bacon. Reversible, the smooth underside can be used for plancha-style cooking.

Cast-iron frying pan with handle, an indispensable accessory for making sauces or melting out fat.

Tumble basket for mounting in the rotisserie – suitable for large vegetables and chestnuts.

Stainless-steel wok, ideal
for stir-frying and sautéing.

Rib rack for ribs
of all kinds – beef,
pork or lamb.

Skewer set for barbecuing juicy shish
kebabs without burning your fingers.

Silicone basting mop for basting slow-cooking cuts, for instance with barbecue sauce.

Silicone basting brush, ideal for glazing spare ribs, for example.

Multi-purpose skewers with ridged ends, perfect for grilling fish or placing food on the barbecue without touching the grid.

Heatproof gloves are more necessary than you think – for right and left hands.

Marinade injectors for injecting meat directly with seasonings, pickling liquid or marinades – saving time and enhancing flavour.

Sandwich toaster, for making creative toasted sandwiches on the barbecue.

Waffle iron, great for using up leftovers.

Microplane fine grater – an essential, even for the barbecue.

Bamboo chopping board with two stainless-steel bowls for catching the meat juices or for collecting chopped vegetables, and knives – the right one for every purpose.

Cranked palette knife, the spatula's little brother.

Bamboo skewers, ideal for yakitori and other barbecued finger food.

Apple corer, but not just for apples.

Grid brush: heat up the grid and then brush clean.

EXTRAS

Grilling plank, from maple to cedar for lovers of subtle smoked flavours. Ideal for cooking food that would otherwise fall apart, stick to the grid, melt (cheese) or fall through the grid. It can also be used for serving, fish for example.

Rotisserie set – whether used with cheese, chicken, cake or suckling pig, the spit holds everything and is always eye-catching.

3-in-1 roasting basket, rib rack and **grilling tray** – for universal use.

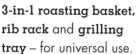

Plancha griddle for French and Spanish-style barbecuing – a versatile accessory for creative barbecuers.

Chimney starter with coconut briquettes.

Pizza stone, perfect for making pizza, tarte flambée and quesadillas.

Tumble basket, for chestnuts, for instance.

Cast-iron frying pan, in action on the Sizzle Zone.

Multi-purpose side compartment for a gas barbecue – although actually designed as a cooler/ice bucket or for storage, you can also cook inside it (see recipe on page 171).

Himalayan salt block, for barbecuing seafood, for instance.

Rotisserie set, can also be used for cakes.

RUMMEL'S ABC OF BARBECUING

A is for accessories

There's a huge selection of accessories to be found on the market. A lot of it is superfluous, in my opinion. A small set of basic accessories is enough to cover any needs (see pages 14–21). When I barbecue, I normally wear black latex gloves because they make it easy to handle everything. And my tongs can't be too long, and they must fit easily in the hand and have an uncomplicated locking mechanism.

B is for burger

When making burgers, there is often the problem of the size ratio of meat to bun. My advice is to make the diameter of the patties up to 20 per cent larger than that of the bun.

C is for charcoal

Charcoal or briquettes? Charcoal is easy to light, so you can get started quickly. Briquettes provide more heat for the barbecue. I recommend charcoal and briquettes made from beech, but briquettes made from coconut shells are also useful. Tip: Beware – not everything marked charcoal has charcoal in it. By the way, in terms of flavour, there is little difference between food cooked using gas or charcoal.

C is for chicken

Unfortunately, chicken too often tends to be overcooked. People often read that for health reasons (salmonella), it has to be cooked to an internal temperature of 70°C/158°F. However, the meat is free of bacteria, completely cooked and juicy with an internal temperature of 60°C/140°F. In any case, salmonella bacteria are – if at all – only found on the surface of the meat, where they are killed off by temperatures of over 100°C/212°F.

C is for chips

Water-soaked wood chips, such as apple or cherry, give food an incomparable smoky flavour.

C is for cleaning the barbecue

The most important tools you need for cleaning are a decent grid brush, a foaming degreaser, a spatula for the drip tray and a cloth. Heat the grid to very hot, then simply give it a good brushing.

C is for cut of meat

The way animals are cut up varies from region to region. Spain and the United States have many cuts that are suitable for barbecuing. America is the home of classic barbecue beef steaks, such as skirt. The French onglet or hanger steak is also great for barbecuing. Such tasty cuts even impress lovers of fillet. I, however, am not a fan of our typical fillet steak, which is a tender enough but tasteless and overpriced cut. From Spain comes presa, shoulder eye, and secreto, skirt, which I consider to be the best pork cuts.

D is for delicious

Food is the raw material I work with. There are no healthy and unhealthy foods as far as I'm concerned. I'm of the opinion that it is the dose that makes the poison. The most important thing for me is that it must be delicious.

D is for dessert

A barbecue just isn't complete without a dessert. I prefer grilled fruit with a lovely combination of toasted flavours, sweetness and a little acidity, together with a creamy sauce and a little added crunch. I'm also partial to serving grilled cheese with fresh fruit.

D is for dry-aged

Dry-ageing involves meat being hung under controlled conditions of temperature and humidity. After about 21 days, it is at its peak tenderness and very aromatic. However, it can also cost up to 1.5 times the price of wet-aged meat.

E is for everyday barbecuing

For me, using the barbecue to prepare food is like using the cooker in the kitchen. It makes no difference whether it's meat or vegetables. Because a barbecue often comes with side burners, which you can use to prepare sauces, for instance, it is highly versatile. Even dishes that are normally cooked in the oven are no problem (see indirect cooking).

I is for improvised vacuum sealing

In the days before I had a professional chamber vacuum sealer, it was always a problem for me to keep meat or vegetables airtight. And ever since I've been cooking with the sous-vide method, I haven't been able to stand air bubbles inside cooking bags. Through experiments, I finally discovered the ziplock bag. You simply fill a tall container with water and then put a steak into a ziplock bag and close the seal, leaving a small opening. By immersing the bag in the water, the water pressure pushes the air out completely, and the bag can be fully sealed. This is what is known in certain circles as my improvised vacuum sealing method.

I is for indirect cooking

Indirect cooking means that the food is not placed directly over embers or a burner. Cooking with indirect heat in a closed barbecue (barbecue with a lid) at an average temperature of 150°C/300°F is similar to cooking in an oven. I generally prefer reverse searing; in other words, I cook my steak to an internal temperature of 55°C/131°F and then sear it over a high heat only to 'paint on' the grid pattern, in order to give it the distinctive toasted flavour.

I is for internal temperature

The following factors influence internal temperature,

Beef (sirloin, rib-eye, onglet, skirt, flank, chuck tender)

rare	medium-rare	medium	medium-well done	well-done
45–50°C	50–55°C	56–58°C	59–65°C	over 65°C
113–122°F	122–131°F	133–136°F	138–149°F	over 149°F

Pork (loin, neck, shoulder eye, skirt, spider steak)

rare	medium-rare	medium	medium-well done	well-done
–	53–55°C	55–60°C	60–65°C	over 65°C
–	127–131°F	131–140°F	140–149°F	over 149°F

Chicken (breast, leg)

rare	medium-rare	medium	medium-well done	well-done
–	–	–	60–65°C	over 65°C
–	–	–	140–149°F	over 149°F

Lamb (loin)

rare	medium-rare	medium	medium-well done	well-done
–	53–55°C	56–60°C	60–65°C	over 65°C
–	127–131°F	133–140°F	140–149°F	over 149°F

Lamb (leg, shoulder)

rare	medium-rare	medium	medium-well done	well-done
–	–	–	60–65°C	over 65°C
–	–	–	140–149°F	over 149°F

and therefore cooking time. When barbecuing, you have to take note of the weight, size and shape of the cuts of meat, whether they are long and thin or small and thick, the amount of marbling, any bones and their size, the type of meat and the amount of connective tissue it contains, and whether it is coated with sauce or marinade. It also depends on whether it will be cooked with direct or indirect heat and how often the lid will be opened. Moreover, the ambient temperature, the temperature of the barbecue and the humidity in it – resulting from the water content of the food – also plays a part. As a general rule, barbecuing is a combination of temperature and time; full heat is never a good thing. A decent barbecue and a meat thermometer are only half of the story. The rest is experience and instinct, and a question of taste and a bit of luck.

M is for Maillard reaction

The Maillard reaction is what causes barbecued food to brown and develop toasted flavours. It begins as soon as the water in the surface areas of the food evaporates. The toasted flavours develop at temperatures above 100°C/212°F, and the actual browning begins at a contact tempera-

ture of 140°C/284°F. The savvy barbecuer aims to quickly form a brown crust without overcooking the meat underneath it – no matter whether the meat is seared beforehand or reverse seared. For this, I either burn the charcoal until it's red-hot, or I use the Sizzle Zone.

M is for marinade

Marinating thin minute steaks makes a lot of sense, but you'll need to resort to other techniques for larger cuts because classic marinades made with oil or dry spice rubs mainly season the surface of the meat. If I want to add flavour to the inside of the meat, I have to soak it in pickling liquid or a brine containing salt and sugar. As an alternative, I recommend the use of marinade injections, which allow the seasonings to penetrate into the meat.

Q is for quality food

It is almost impossible to tell from the packaging whether, even with meticulous preparation, you will end up with a tasty and juicy piece of meat on your plate. Terms like 'farm fresh' are merely imaginative branding. Even an organic label says nothing about the flavour. Factors such as the sex of the animal, its date of slaughter, what it was fed, its type of rearing and the ageing of the meat play a big part, but providing this information isn't the norm. My advice is look for a butcher you can trust or ask the people staffing the supermarket meat counter the relevant questions. Then buy a cut, cook it properly on the barbecue and try it. Draw your own conclusions for the next time.

R is for resting

Meat needs resting to prevent the juices from leaking out when cut. When heated, the muscles contract and squeeze out the juices. By resting the meat, the proteins in the meat juices thicken again. It is enough to rest the meat for 5-10 minutes on a rack in a warm place. If wrapped in aluminium foil, the meat will not cool evenly and steam will condense on the foil, which will also ruin the crust on the meat.

S is for sealing meat

There is a stubbornly persistent legend that searing meat over a high heat seals its pores, keeping in the juices. However, meat has no pores to be able to seal. In fact, prolonged high heat causes the collagen in the meat to shrink, squeezing out the juices. The evidence of this is the hiss you hear when searing meat, and the red liquid on the surface of the meat and juices trickling onto the plate before a cooked steak is even sliced, whether or not it has been seared.

S is for Sizzle Zone

Meat cooked sous-vide or using the reverse searing method is still missing the toasted flavours, so it needs to be seared over a high heat. The infrared side burner, the Sizzle Zone, is ideal for this. At a temperature of over 800°C/1472°F, I can quickly achieve the toasted flavours I want without raising the internal temperature. For barbecues without a Sizzle Zone, I recommend pre-heating a cast iron griddle plate to a high temperature.

S is for smoking

Smoking is an indirect form of barbecuing at low temperature (70-140°C/158-284°F), mainly of large cuts of meat, with infused smoke over a long period of time (4-24 hours). A typical smoker is the water smoker, but you can also use a commercially available barbecue that comes with a lid.

S is for sous-vide cooking

I find the benefits of sous-vide cooking to be obvious. The food is seasoned in the bag with herbs, spices and oils. Because of this, the meat stays juicy and tender and the degree of doneness can be controlled more precisely. I have included two recipes on pages 48 and 72 which require the use of a sous-vide machine. If you don't have one sadly you won't be able to create these dishes.

S is for starter chimney

It is used for lighting charcoal or briquettes. Particularly when cooking for several hours, place

glowing coals inside. It is also ideal for cooking with a wok.

S is for steak

You often hear that a steak should be taken out of the fridge 2 hours before cooking in order to bring it to room temperature, so that it doesn't suffer from thermal shock and so it stays juicy. However, this makes spontaneous barbecuing practically impossible. I wonder if this thermal shock is really minimised if the steak at 20°C/68°F instead of 5°C/41°F is put onto a barbecue heated to 300°C/572°F.

So, whenever I feel like a steak, I take it out of the fridge, season it with a pinch of salt and wait 10–15 minutes while the barbecue heats up. Then I cook the steak by turning it over constantly – every 25 seconds – until it reaches an internal temperature of 55°C/131°F. Now it only needs a little resting, and then bon appétit!

U is for umami

This Japanese word is used to refer to one of the five basic tastes, together with sweet, sour, salty and bitter. It is a generic term for savoury flavours and is found in glutamate-rich foods such as Parmesan cheese and dried tomatoes.

V is for vegetarian

I'm convinced that people would eat more vegetarian food if they knew how to prepare vegetables better. Water is the worst enemy of many kinds of vegetables because it causes their flavour to leach out. Vegetables mostly comprise water, around which there is a little flavour. It is necessary to reduce their water content when barbecuing, concentrating their flavour and texture, which can be enhanced with salt, spices and butter or olive oil.

W is for winter barbecues

There are a number of things to bear in mind when barbecuing in winter. In cold weather, a lid is essential to create and maintain a workable temperature.

You should also keep an eye on the gas. The gas bottles often used with portable barbecues have a higher proportion of butane. This mixture makes barbecuing at temperatures under 5°C/41°F practically impossible. This isn't a problem with propane. However, it's also possible for the gas bottle to freeze in this case if all the burners are running at full steam on a large barbecue. There are devices available that can connect two bottles together so that the barbecue draws gas out of both at the same time.

When planning your time, bear in mind that larger cuts of meat may need to be cooked longer in the cold. In order to avoid having to lift the lid unnecessarily, I recommend the use of a probe thermometer. As for choice of food, when it comes to winter barbecues, I'm a great fan of food you eat with your hands, such as burgers, wraps and skewers. It's practical because your guests can stand and it's quicker to eat. Bear in mind that sauces can freeze in the cold. A cooler containing a heat pack (an ice pack warmed in hot water) can be a practical solution.

I prefer to have hot side dishes – you can also warm your fingers with a baked potato. China or glass plates should be warmed beforehand, or you can use disposable tableware, made from wood or sugar cane, for instance. For drinks, you can use the barbecue as a heated bar, with pots holding drinks such as mulled wine, hot caipirinhas or fruit juice. Naturally, there should be dessert. Baked apples or grilled bananas don't require great effort and are a great way to round off a winter barbecue meal. When barbecuing in the darkest season of the year, lighting the barbecue is important. Some models come with integrated lighting, and there are spotlights that can be attached to the lid as accessories. Otherwise, it is important to light the area around the barbecue. I also recommend an infrared heater as a source of light and heat.

X is for Xmas

Barbecuing has a place at Christmas. New accessories, interesting books and vouchers for courses are gifts that will make any barbecue enthusiasts happy. Festive menu suggestions can be found on page 216.

SEASONAL CALENDAR

FISH AND SEAFOOD

Even fish should be bought seasonally. This is in order to protect species, but also because some fish, such as herring, taste different depending on the season. Matjes, soused herrings, are made in early summer, when herring are relatively fat but have not yet begun to reproduce. Atlantic mackerel, on the other hand, are tastiest in autumn, when they have recovered after spawning. They are somewhat lean in spring, fasting over the winter in deep water.

Species listed (left table): Anchovy, European; Arctic char; Atlantic catfish; Atlantic mackerel; Brown crab; Brown shrimp; Carp; Cockle; Cod; Crayfish; Eel, European; Flatfish; Garfish; Gilthead bream; Grey mullet; Haddock; Hake; Halibut; Herring; King scallop; King crab; Langoustine; Lobster; Monkfish; Mussel; Octopus, squid, cuttlefish; Oyster; Pangasius catfish (basa); Perch, European; Pike; Pollack, saithe; Red mullet; Red snapper; Rosefish.

Species listed (right table): Sardine; Sea bass, European; Sea snails; Sea urchin; Shark; Skate; Sturgeon; Swordfish; Tiger prawn; Tilapia; Trout; Tub gurnard; Tuna; Turbot; Venus clam; Wedge-shell (tellin) clam; Wels catfish; Zander.

Months: Jan, Feb, Mar, Apr, May, Jun, Jul, Aug, Sep, Oct, Nov, Dec.

Legend:
- Available
- High Season
- Not Available

FRUIT AND VEGETABLES

t's obvious that I prefer seasonal produce. It's good for he environment because it's mainly grown locally, and t tastes better because it's allowed to ripen and it comes o market freshly harvested.
t's even better if you have an organic producer nearby.

Fresh
Cold Storage
Fresh and Cold Storage
Local Not Available

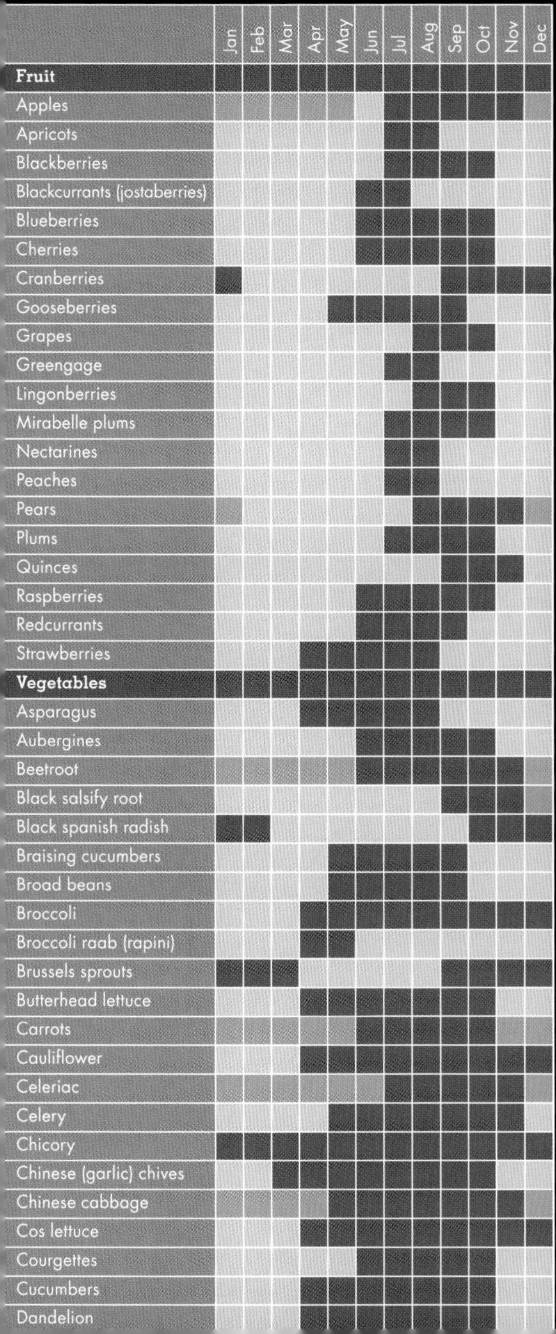

Jan
Feb
Mar
Apr
May
Jun
Jul
Aug
Sep
Oct
Nov
Dec
Fruit
Apples
Apricots
Blackberries
Blackcurrants (jostaberries)
Blueberries
Cherries
Cranberries
Gooseberries
Grapes
Greengage
Lingonberries
Mirabelle plums
Nectarines
Peaches
Pears
Plums
Quinces
Raspberries
Redcurrants
Strawberries
Vegetables
Asparagus
Aubergines
Beetroot
Black salsify root
Black spanish radish
Braising cucumbers
Broad beans
Broccoli
Broccoli raab (rapini)
Brussels sprouts
Butterhead lettuce
Carrots
Cauliflower
Celeriac
Celery
Chicory
Chinese (garlic) chives
Chinese cabbage
Cos lettuce
Courgettes
Cucumbers
Dandelion

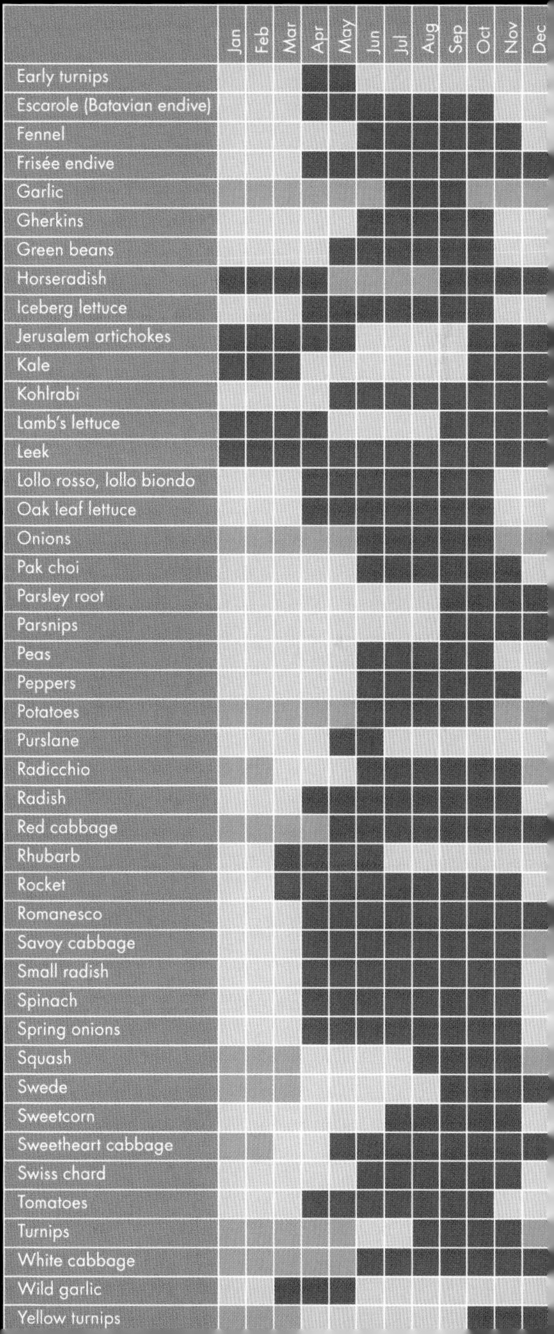

Jan
Feb
Mar
Apr
May
Jun
Jul
Aug
Sep
Oct
Nov
Dec
Early turnips
Escarole (Batavian endive)
Fennel
Frisée endive
Garlic
Gherkins
Green beans
Horseradish
Iceberg lettuce
Jerusalem artichokes
Kale
Kohlrabi
Lamb's lettuce
Leek
Lollo rosso, lollo biondo
Oak leaf lettuce
Onions
Pak choi
Parsley root
Parsnips
Peas
Peppers
Potatoes
Purslane
Radicchio
Radish
Red cabbage
Rhubarb
Rocket
Romanesco
Savoy cabbage
Small radish
Spinach
Spring onions
Squash
Swede
Sweetcorn
Sweetheart cabbage
Swiss chard
Tomatoes
Turnips
White cabbage
Wild garlic
Yellow turnips

LET'S GET FIRED UP

RECIPES

BEEF

More than any other food, a slab of beef symbolises the masculine side of barbecuing. What would a decent barbecue be without a perfectly cooked steak that only needs a little salt and perhaps a sprinkling of freshly ground pepper? Beef is always a treat: flash seared over a very high heat as tataki, in the form of a classic burger, or as a rare or medium steak – well done is unthinkable! Or brisket, slow-cooked in the traditional American sense of barbecue, in a smoker. Cuts like chuck, onglet and flank steaks today make the hearts of meat connoisseurs beat faster, but it has been a long journey. Together with pigs, cattle were the first animals to be domesticated by humans, who used them as working animals and to supply them with meat and milk. Cattle today are almost exclusively reared for meat and milk. Because of this, there is increasing reliance on breeds that are suitable for meat production, which include Black Angus, Hereford, Limousin, Charolais, Simmental, Wagyu and Belgian Blue. Chianina, the largest cattle in the world, are a typical example of how cattle bred as draught animals have over the years developed into a breed reared exclusively for meat.

RIBS

ONGLET

STEAK

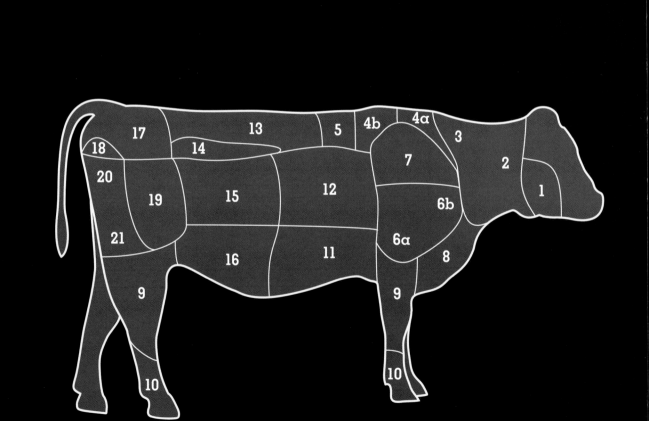

THE BEST CUTS

Culinary globalisation hasn't stopped at the different cuts of meat. After BSE had largely disappeared from consumer consciousness, in the early twenty-first century, fillet or sirloin steaks were once again cooked on the barbecue – although usually only for special guests. In the meantime, the demand for flavourful, high-quality meat has been growing steadily in Europe, (the ever-growing barbecue scene has played a considerable part in this). This has primarily been covered by imports from America, Canada and Ireland. South American meat is also very popular, although my opinion is that it doesn't taste as good as the meat from the previously mentioned countries. This influx of meat not only brought well-known cuts such as beef fillet and sirloin, but also others which from a European perspective were considered to be taken from inferior parts of the animal and not suitable for short cooking methods. However, the opposite is now happening. Tasty cuts such as flank and skirt are becoming increasingly popular. I have also been on a quest to find little-known but delicious cuts that are juicy and tender when properly prepared.

Considerable success has been achieved in recent years in the rearing of high-quality beef cattle. It hasn't been enough just to rear animals that taste good, but there have also been positive developments in terms of methods of slaughtering and processing, i.e. ageing the meat.

For local barbecuers, however, it is still difficult to find high-quality beef nationwide. And where it is available, it takes a trained eye to recognise it. A traceable meat quality assessment system for the consumer, such as those found in America or Australia, would be very helpful in my opinion.

You won't find cuts such as porterhouse, T-bone or tomahawk steaks in this book. When you buy cuts like these, you're actually purchasing beef bones for a very high price. Aside from that, the bones prevent uniform heating of the meat; they also absorb heat, so the meat around the bone takes longer to reach the desired internal temperature.

There's also another rationale to justify these sorts of steaks: an animal has higher value added if you can sell its bones at the price of a steak, instead of processing them elsewhere.

How the 'perfect steak' is meant to look and be prepared is an important subject in its own right – you could write a whole book on this topic alone.

A number of tips and tricks have already been given on pages 22-25.

FLAVOUR

Beef tastes a little salty – the term umami is also a suitable description – with a slight sweetness and acidity, as long as it isn't overcooked. Its flavour also depends on how it is aged: dry-aged meat tastes nutty, whereas lean wet-aged meat often has a very metallic taste. Beef has a special relationship with spicy ingredients, such as mustard, horseradish and chilli, but it also goes well with pears (Korean bulgogi p.44), coconut and tomato. In addition to traditional herbs like rosemary and thyme, beef also combines well with dill, watercress, coriander and mint. Other suitable aromatics include cinnamon, ginger and coffee.

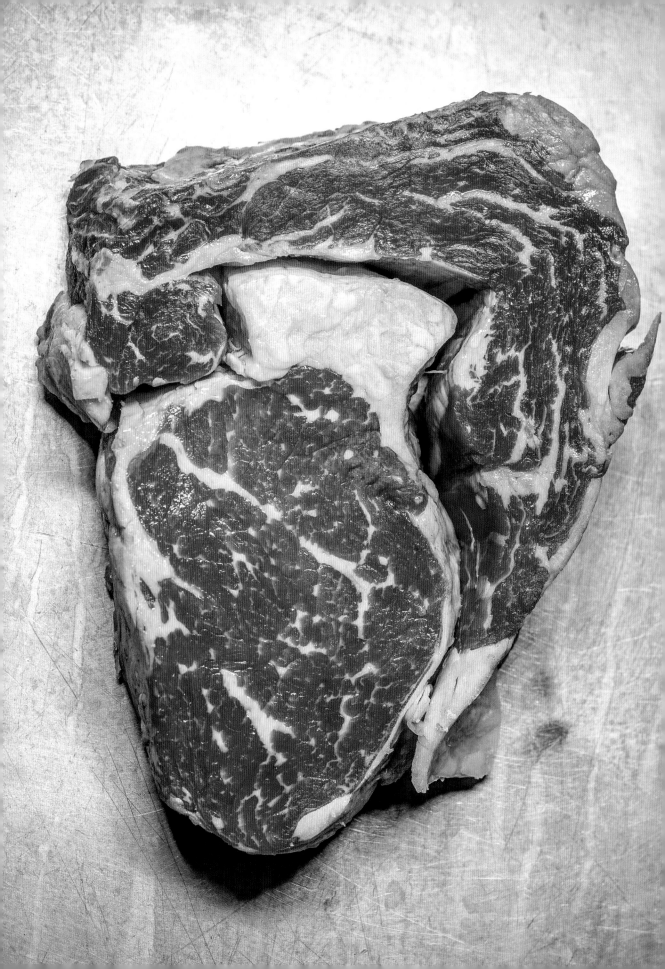

DECONSTRUCTED
RIB-EYE

Rib-eye steak consists of several muscles, the largest of which are the *longissimus dorsi* and *spinalis dorsi*. The former, the loin muscle or rib loin, extends forward from the sirloin as part of the muscles of the back, which sit to the right and left of the backbone and provide support. The latter, which forms a kind of lid for the former – hence the name rib-eye cap – belongs to the muscles of the respiratory system and is therefore constantly in motion. As a rule, I separate the two parts of the rib-eye and prepare either the loin or the cap. I believe the rib-eye cap to be the best cut of beef, the most noble part.

RIB-EYE CAP

SERVES 4 AS A MAIN COURSE
READY IN: 20 MINUTES
DIFFICULTY: ✪✪✧

1 (about 800 g/1¾ lb) rib-eye cap, cut from the rib-eye
Fermented black pepper
Sea salt

1. Trim the rib-eye cap and lay on a hot grid. Cook for 7–10 minutes until the internal temperature of the meat reaches 55°C/131°F, turning over every 30 seconds.

2. Cut the meat into portions, season with salt and pepper, and serve.

RIB LOIN

SERVES 4 AS A MAIN COURSE
READY IN: 1 HOUR
DIFFICULTY: ✪✪✧

800 g/1¾ lb rib loin
Salt

1. Cut the meat into 4-cm/1½-inch-thick steaks and reverse sear. See page 23 for instructions on reverse searing by indirect cooking to reach 55°C/131°F. This can take up to 45 minutes.

2. Season with salt being serving.

ROAST BEEF
TATAKI

SERVES 4 AS A STARTER
READY IN: 30 MINUTES
DIFFICULTY: ✪ ✪ ✪

1 clove garlic
Grated zest 1 untreated lemon
Freshly ground pepper
200 g/7 oz sirloin
50 g/⅔ cup freshly grated Parmesan cheese
2 tbsp olive oil
Salt

1. Peel and halve the garlic clove. Rub a serving dish with the garlic. Sprinkle the dish with lemon zest and pepper.

2. Sear the meat on all sides over a high heat. The centre should remain uncooked and only the surface browned for a toasted flavour. Take the meat off the barbecue. Use a sharp knife to cut into very thin slices as for carpaccio.

3. Smooth out the slices or flatten with a meat tenderiser and arrange over the serving dish. Season the tataki with salt and pepper. Sprinkle with the grated Parmesan and drizzle with the olive oil.

I prefer to use the topside end of the sirloin, seeing as it can't be cut into nice steaks.

SPIDER STEAK
WITH FENNEL

SERVES 4 AS A MAIN COURSE
READY IN: 30 MINUTES
DIFFICULTY: ✪✪✪

2 fennel bulbs
2 tbsp olive oil
Juice ½ lemon
2 tbsp unsalted butter
4 sprigs thyme, plucked
2 spider steaks (200–250 g/7–9 oz each)
Salt, freshly ground pepper

1. Peel off the hard outer layer from the fennel bulbs and cut into 1–2-cm/½-¾-in-thick slices. Lightly season with salt and leave to stand for 5 minutes. Coat with some of the olive oil and cook directly on both sides for 5 minutes over a moderate heat until light sear marks appear. Transfer the fennel to the indirect cooking side of the barbecue and cook for 20 more minutes at 120°C/250°F.

2. Combine the lemon juice, butter, thyme and the rest of the oil in an aluminium container and warm on the barbecue.

3. In the meantime, cook the meat directly on the hot side of the barbecue for about 6 minutes, turning over every 30 seconds and regularly checking the internal temperature. When it reaches 55°C/131°F, take the meat off the heat and rest for 5 minutes.

4. When it is time to serve, cut the meat into slices and arrange over the fennel. Season the meat and fennel with salt and pepper and drizzle with the warm lemon juice, olive oil and butter mixture.

Spider steak is little known, but whether it comes from a cow or a pig, it is a very flavourful cut. Beef spider steak is oval in shape, about 1 cm/½ in thick and the size of your palm, and it is cut from inside the hip bone of the animal. It should be available to order from good butchers. You can also source it from certain Internet sites.

RUMP STEAK
BAGUETTE SANDWICH

SERVES 4 AS A MAIN COURSE
READY IN: 1 HOUR
DIFFICULTY: ✪✪✪

500 g/1¼ lb shallots
2 tsp icing sugar
2 tbsp unsalted butter
100 ml/scant ½ cup dry red wine
½ tsp thyme leaves, plus extra to garnish
Salt, freshly ground pepper
1 kg/2¼ lb rump steak
1 baguette
2 tomatoes
1 head cos lettuce

FOR THE MAYONNAISE

3 tbsp mayonnaise
2 tsp wholegrain mustard
1 dash lemon juice
Salt, freshly ground pepper

1. Peel and halve the shallots lengthways.

2. Melt the icing sugar in a griddle pan, add the butter and shallots, and briefly caramelise. Deglaze the pan with the wine and add the thyme. Cook the shallots for about 15 minutes, stirring from time to time, until soft and the wine is reduced by half. Season with salt and pepper.

3. While the shallots are cooking, halve the steak lengthways and sear both pieces on all sides on the hot barbecue. Transfer the meat to the indirect cooking side and cook at about 120°C/250°F until the internal temperature reaches 57°C/135°F. Take off the barbecue and rest in a warm place for 5 minutes.

4. In the meantime, halve the baguette lengthways and set aside the top half. Cut the tomatoes into 1-cm-/½-in-thick slices and separate the lettuce leaves. Sear both the tomatoes and lettuce leaves quickly until sear marks appear. Mix all the ingredients for the mayonnaise together.

5. Toast the bottom half of the baguette on its cut side, then spread with the mayonnaise. Cover with tomato and lettuce. Cut the meat into about 5-mm/¼-in-thick slices and add a generous serving to the baguette. Season with salt and pepper. Top with the warm shallots and garnish with a few thyme leaves. Cover the baguette with the top half and cut the sandwich into bite-sized pieces.

PHILLY CHEESESTEAK SANDWICH

SERVES 4 AS A MAIN COURSE
READY IN: 45 MINUTES
DIFFICULTY: ✪ ✪ ✪

800 g/1¾ lb hanger steak
150–200 g/5–7 oz provolone cheese
1 Spanish onion
2 tbsp teriyaki sauce
4 slices toasting bread
Salt, freshly ground pepper

This recipe makes use of a maple or cedar grilling plank. Both meat and cheese acquire an incomparably delicate smoked flavour.

1. Trim the meat and cut the fatty trimmings into small dice. Put the trimmings into a cast-iron frying pan over the side burner and melt the fat.

2. Cut the cheese into two 2–3-cm/¾–1¼-in-thick slices and set aside. Peel and finely slice the onion. Fry the onion in the pan with the melted fat until brown, then deglaze the pan with the teriyaki sauce and set aside.

3. Heat the barbecue to 120°C/250°F and cook the meat with indirect heat until its internal temperature reaches 53°C/127°F. Lay the cheese on a maple or cedar grilling plank and place directly over the working burner of the barbecue. The plank will start to smoke, flavouring both meat and cheese, and the cheese will begin to melt.

4. Take the meat off the barbecue and set aside in a warm place. Turn up the heat of the barbecue to the highest setting. Return the steak to the barbecue and sear each side for 20 seconds until sear marks develop, giving it a toasted flavour (if you have a Napoleon barbecue with a Sizzle Zone, you can take the meat straight from the cooking area and immediately sear it there).

5. In the meantime, toast the bread and spread with the onion. Cut the meat into thin slices, season with salt and pepper, and place over the onion on the bread. Top with the soft cheese and serve.

FLANK STEAK
AND GUACAMOLE ROLLS

SERVES 4 AS A STARTER
READY IN: 30 MINUTES
DIFFICULTY: ✪✪✪

800 g/1¾ lb flank steaks
1 ear corn on the cob
Salt
1 tsp unsalted butter
1 beef tomato
4 (18-cm/7-in diameter) tortillas
Finely chopped coriander, to garnish
1 tbsp sesame seeds, to garnish
2 spring onions, cut in fine rings,
    to garnish

FOR THE GUACAMOLE

2 avocados
Juice of ½ lime
3 tsp chopped coriander
1 medium red onion, finely diced
½ red chilli pepper, de-seeded and finely
    diced
Salt

1. Lightly season the steaks on both sides and set aside for 10 minutes. Lightly salt the corn, coat with butter and barbecue at 150°C/300°F until light sear marks appear. Remove from the barbecue, leave to cool and cut off the kernels.

2. For the guacamole, halve the avocados and remove the stone. Scoop out the flesh into a bowl and crush with a fork. Mix in the other ingredients. Add the corn kernels.

3. Sear the steaks for 5–10 minutes over a very high heat, maximum power, turning over every 30 seconds. They are done when their internal temperature reaches 56°C/133°F. Check the temperature for the first time after 4 minutes, so that you can estimate the remaining cooking time. Take the meat off the barbecue and set aside in a warm place.

4. Halve the tomato, scoop out the seeds and discard. Cut the flesh into 1-cm/½-in-thick rings, and then into strips. Trim the tortillas on four sides to form a square (12–14-cm/4½–5½-in sides) and lay side by side on the work surface.

5. Slice the meat against the grain into about 1-cm/½-in-thick strips. Spread a band of about 3 tablespoons guacamole along one edge of each tortilla and lightly fold the tortilla to cover. Alternate two strips of meat with two tomato strips on the tortilla and roll up completely. Lay the wraps on the barbecue on their meat side to give a toasted flavour and make crispy. The guacamole should remain cold.

6. Cut the tortillas into 3-cm/1¼-in lengths and garnish with coriander, a pinch of sesame seeds and spring onion rings.

BULGOGI

SERVES 4 AS A STARTER
MARINATING TIME: 4 HOURS
READY IN: 30 MINUTES
DIFFICULTY: ✪✪○

---

400 g/14 oz sirloin
Salt
3 carrots
5 mini cucumbers
1 tbsp salt
1 tbsp sugar
2 tbsp rice vinegar
5-cm/2-in mooli
1 head cos lettuce

FOR THE MARINADE

2 pears
Juice and zest 1 untreated lemon
2 tbsp rice wine
1 tsp sesame oil
1 tsp sesame seeds
1 clove garlic
2 tbsp soy sauce
1 tsp sugar
1 pinch salt

1. Cut the meat into 1-cm/½-in-thick, bite-sized strips and lightly season with salt on both sides.

2. For the marinade, coarsely grate the pears and mix well with the other ingredients in a bowl. Add the meat, coat well in the marinade and marinate in the refrigerator for 4 hours.

3. Use a mandoline slicer to finely shave the carrots and cucumbers and mix in a bowl with the salt, sugar and vinegar. Finely shave the mooli and spread over a chopping board in order to allow the hot mustard oil it contains to dissipate a little. Separate, wash and pat dry the lettuce leaves. Arrange the carrot, cucumber and mooli shavings on top of the lettuce leaves, which can be rolled up.

4. Take the meat out of the marinade and pat dry. Cook on the barbecue over a high heat on both sides for no longer than 2 minutes, turning over twice in this time. Arrange the meat over the salad and serve.

Bulgogi, which means 'fire meat', is a Korean-style barbecue dish.

SIRLOIN
WITH BREAD SALAD

SERVES 4 AS A MAIN COURSE
READY IN: 45 MINUTES
DIFFICULTY: ❶❷❸

800 g/1¾ lb sirloin
1 bunch thyme
1 bunch basil
1 bunch parsley
100 g/3¾ oz white bread
100 g/3¾ oz brown (mixed wheat and
   rye) bread
4 firm tomatoes
1 red onion
Salt
Olive oil, to serve
Parmesan cheese, to serve
Freshly ground pepper

FOR THE DRESSING
100 ml/scant ½ cup olive oil
2 tbsp red wine vinegar
1 tsp mustard
Salt, freshly ground pepper

1. Trim the meat. Cut the fatty trimmings into small dice and put into a cast-iron frying pan. Cut the trimmed meat into four steaks of equal size and season with a pinch of salt on each side. Cook the steaks with indirect heat for about 40 minutes at about 110°C/230°F, until the internal temperature reaches 55°C/131°F, turning over twice in this time.

2. Place the pan with the fat directly over the heat, add the thyme and melt the fat. Dip the steaks regularly in the fat as they cook.

3. Mix together the ingredients for the dressing and season with a pinch of salt and pepper. Finely chop the basil and parsley leaves.

4. Cut both types of bread into 3–4-cm/1¼–1½-in cubes and mix with 2–3 tablespoons of the dressing. Thread the cubes of bread onto skewers and toast directly over the heat, turning over several times. Halve the tomatoes vertically and cook directly over their cut side for 5 minutes.

5. Peel and cut the onion into fine strips and put into a bowl. Take the tomatoes off the barbecue and dice. Take the bread off the skewers and mix with the tomatoes, chopped herbs and the remaining dressing in the bowl with the onions.

6. Take the meat off the barbecue, set aside in a warm place and raise the heat. Sear the steaks twice on both sides on the hot grid, for about 30 seconds each, rotating them 45° with each turn to leave decorative sear marks. Cut the meat into 1–2-cm/½–¾-in-thick strips and arrange over the bread salad. Season with salt and pepper, drizzle with a few drops of olive oil and top with a few Parmesan shavings.

BEEF CHEEK
SKEWERS

SERVES 4 AS A MAIN COURSE
SOUS-VIDE COOKING TIME: 36 HOURS
READY IN: 45 MINUTES
DIFFICULTY: ✪✪✪

---

4 beef cheeks

4 tbsp barbecue seasoning
   (e.g. basic spice rub on page 211)

200 ml/scant 1 cup basic barbecue sauce
   (see page 206)

EQUIPMENT
Sous-vide machine

1. Trim the cheeks and rub with the seasoning. Vacuum seal the meat inside a bag and cook sous-vide for 36 hours at 63°C/145°F.

2. Open the bag, take out the meat, pat dry and pierce each cheek with a skewer. Position the skewers on the barbecue at about 120°C/250°F for 30 minutes and glaze with the barbecue sauce, brushing with the sauce several times.

SHORT RIBS

SERVES 4 AS A MAIN COURSE
READY IN: 8 HOURS
DIFFICULTY: ✪✪✪

4 short ribs each 300 g/11 oz
1 apple
100 g/2 cups barbecue seasoning
  (e.g. basic spice rub on page 211)
2 tsp thyme leaves
3 sprigs rosemary
2 tbsp unsalted butter
200 ml/scant 1 cup basic barbecue sauce
  (see page 206)

1. Trim the ribs and scrape the membrane off the bones. Core and slice the apple.

2. Rub the ribs with a generous amount of the seasoning. Wrap together with the thyme, rosemary, apple slices and butter in aluminium foil and cook with indirect heat at 120°C/250°F for about 5 hours.
Take the ribs off the barbecue and unwrap.

3. If possible, attach a smoking tube to the barbecue and smoke the ribs for 2 hours at a maximum temperature of 100°C/212°F. Brush the meat regularly with the barbecue sauce as it smokes.

Short ribs are cut from the very fatty ribs of the breast area. The different rib cuts are gaining in popularity.

TERES MAJOR

SERVES 4 AS A MAIN COURSE
READY IN: 1 HOUR
DIFFICULTY: ✪○○

2 teres major steaks (about 600 g/1 lb 6 oz each)
Salt, freshly ground pepper

1. Cook the meat with indirect heat at about 100°C/212°F until its internal temperature reaches 55°C/131°F, which should take about 50 minutes.

2. Sear the steaks on the infrared side burner (Sizzle Zone), then season with salt and pepper, and serve. Alternatively, sear the meat on the barbecue and set aside in a warm place. The barbecue must be at a very high heat and the meat flash seared until it develops attractive char marks. Then season with salt and pepper. Slice to serve.

COUNTRY-STYLE BREAD WITH LAMB'S LETTUCE AND TAFELSPITZ

SERVES 4 AS A MAIN COURSE
READY IN: 1 HOUR 30 MINUTES
DIFFICULTY: ✪✪○

1 (about 800 g/1¾ lb) tafelspitz (cut from the rump cap)
Salt
100 ml/scant ½ cup pumpkin seed oil
100 ml/scant ½ cup beef stock
1 pinch mustard
1 tsp lemon juice
1 tbsp soy sauce
4 thick slices country-style brown (rye) bread
100 g/2½ cups lamb's lettuce

FOR THE HORSERADISH SAUCE

1 untreated lemon
250 g/1 cup yoghurt
2 tbsp freshly grated horseradish
1 tbsp olive oil
4–6 sprigs thyme, plucked
1 apple
Salt, freshly ground pepper

1. Score the fatty side of the tafelspitz in a cross-hatch pattern, then lightly salt the meat all over. Cook the meat with indirect heat at 120°C/250°F for about 1 hour until the internal temperature reaches 55°C/131°F. Then sear the fatty side on a cast-iron griddle plate over direct heat to melt the fat and form a crust.

2. In the meantime, make a vinaigrette by mixing the oil with the stock, mustard, lemon juice and soy sauce.

3. For the sauce, grate the lemon zest and squeeze the juice. Mix the zest and juice together with the other ingredients for the horseradish sauce, except the apple. Wash and cut the apple into julienne strips and mix with the sauce. Spread the slices of bread with the sauce and cover with the lamb's lettuce.

4. Take the meat off the barbecue, slice and arrange over the vegetables. Drizzle the meat with the vinaigrette.

TAGLIATA WITH ONGLET STEAK

SERVES 4 AS A STARTER
READY IN: 30 MINUTES
DIFFICULTY: ✪✪✪

700 g/1 lb 9 oz onglet (hanger) steak
Salt
1 red onion
2 carrots
Olive oil
1 bunch rocket
12 cherry tomatoes
1 clove garlic

FOR THE DRESSING

50 g/⅔ cup coarsely grated Parmesan
    cheese
3 tbsp olive oil
2 tbsp balsamic vinegar
2 tsp wholegrain Dijon mustard
Salt, freshly ground pepper

1. Lightly salt the meat on both sides and set aside for 15 minutes.

2. Peel the onion and carrots. Finely dice the onion and slice the carrots. Sauté both ingredients separately with a little oil in a cast-iron frying pan over a high heat – 5 minutes for the onion and 8 minutes for the carrots.

3. In the meantime, wash the rocket and shake dry. Wash the tomatoes. Peel and finely chop the garlic. Mix the tomatoes with the garlic, onion and carrots in a bowl, then mix in the rocket. Mix together all the ingredients for the dressing and dress the salad.

4. Sear the meat over a high heat on the barbecue for 5 minutes, turning over every 30 seconds until its internal temperature reaches 55°C/131°F. Immediately slice the meat and arrange over the salad, allowing the meat juices to run into the salad.

The name of this dish, tagliata, comes from the Italian word meaning sliced. The cut of meat from the diaphragm is known by its French name, onglet, or hanger steak, and is also known in America as hanging tenderloin.

RUMMEL BURGER 2.0

SERVES 4 AS A MAIN COURSE
START 2 DAYS BEFORE
READY IN: 2 HOURS 46 MINUTES
DIFFICULTY: ✪✪✩

---

8 eggs
500 g/1¼ lb minced beef (20% fat)
Salt, freshly ground pepper
100 g/1 cup grated Cheddar cheese
1 ciabatta loaf, cut into 4 equal lengths

FOR THE GARNISH

3 red onions
1 pear
2 spring onions
Salt, freshly ground pepper
Olive oil
3 tbsp finely chopped sun-dried tomatoes
50 g/½ cup crumbled Roquefort (or other
   blue) cheese
1 tsp lemon juice
2 tbsp mayonnaise

I'm a big fan of the stuffed burger.
When it comes to the fillings, you
can pretty much let your creativity
run wild.

1. Freeze the eggs 2 days before making the burgers. Take the eggs out of the freezer 2 hours before and thaw in a bowl filled with warm water.

2. Take the mince out of the fridge immediately before making the burgers as it should be very cold. Alternatively, you can chill the meat in the freezer for 30 minutes. Season the meat with salt and pepper and prepare four stuffed burgers with a burger press. To do this, fill the burger press with half of the mince and press down, forming a large well.

3. Separate the eggs. The egg yolks should resemble waxy balls. Put two egg yolks into each well and fill the rest of the space with grated cheese. Cover with the rest of the mince and press to form the burgers. Use the egg whites in another recipe.

4. For the garnish, peel and cut the red onions into julienne strips and put into a bowl. Peel and quarter the pear. Grate one quarter and add to the bowl. Thinly slice the spring onions and mix with the other ingredients in the bowl. Lightly season the mixture with salt and pepper, and add a little olive oil and the tomatoes. Mix in the cheese and lemon juice.

5. Cook each burger on both sides for 3 minutes over a medium heat. Then transfer to the indirect cooking side of the barbecue and leave to stand for 10 minutes. Lightly toast the bread, cut open across the middle and spread the cut sides with mayonnaise. Lay the burger on the bottom half, garnish with the cheese and onion topping and cover with the top half of the bread.

RAMEN BURGER

SERVES 4 AS A MAIN COURSE
READY IN: 45 MINUTES
DIFFICULTY: ✪✪✪

4 packets instant ramen noodles
2 eggs
3 tbsp peanut oil
600 g/1 lb 6 oz minced beef (at least 20% fat)
3 tbsp mayonnaise
4 tbsp basic barbecue sauce (see page 206)
Salt, freshly ground pepper
Tomato, gherkins, red onion, etc. to garnish (optional)

ACCESSORIES
4 x 12-cm/4½-in ring moulds

1. Prepare the noodles according to the instructions on the packet. Set aside the spice sachets. Put the cooked noodles into a sieve and leave to drain for 3 minutes. Beat the eggs in a bowl, add the noodles and mix well.

2. Grease the ring moulds. Heat a griddle plate on the barbecue and add a little peanut oil. Lay the rings on the griddle. Fill each ring with ⅛th of the noodles, press firmly and add a weight. Fry the noodles for 3 minutes, then carefully lift off the rings. Turn the noodle discs and fry for 3 more minutes. Repeat the process to make eight noodle discs. Keep warm.

3. Make four 2-cm/¾-in-thick and 12-cm/4½-in-diameter burgers from the mince. Press down on the centre of each to make a well, it will stop the burgers puffing up. Cook the burgers as preferred – rare, medium or well-done.

4. Season the mayonnaise with a sachet of ramen spices and spread the noodle discs with the mayonnaise. Place a burger on a noodle disc. Cover with barbecue sauce, season with salt and pepper, and top with a garnish of choice. Cover with a second noodle disc and enjoy.

MAC 'N' CHEESE CALZONE

SERVES 4 AS A MAIN COURSE
READY IN: 30 MINUTES
DIFFICULTY: ✪✪✪

400 ml/1²/₃ cups milk
200 g/2 cups macaroni
50 g/½ cup each of Cheddar, Gouda and
    mozzarella cheese, finely diced
1 package pizza dough (from the
    refrigerated section of a supermarket)
    approx. 200 g/7 oz
Spray oil
100 g/½ cup salami, cut into fine strips
Basil
2 tomatoes, finely diced

1. Bring the milk to the boil in a pan. Cook the pasta in the boiling milk for about 10 minutes until al dente. Take the pan off the heat, stir the cheese into the pasta and leave to melt.

2. Cut the pizza dough into eight equal squares to fit a sandwich toaster – for me this is 16 x 16 cm/6¼ x 6¼ in – with an additional margin of 1 cm/½ in.

3. Spray the inside of the sandwich toaster with oil and lay one dough square inside. Cover with 2 tablespoons of salami strips and 3–4 tablespoons of mac and cheese. Top with a couple of basil leaves and 1 tablespoon of diced tomato, and then cover with a second dough square.

4. Close the sandwich toaster well and toast in the barbecue with indirect heat at 200°C/400°F for 3 minutes. Open the sandwich toaster and carefully transfer the calzone to a plate. Repeat the process to make three more.

Top left: Portobello Sandwich
Top right: Onion Burger
Bottom: Mac 'n' Cheese Calzone

ONION BURGER

SERVES 4 AS A MAIN COURSE
READY IN: 2 HOURS 45 MINUTES
DIFFICULTY: ✪✪✪

4 Spanish onions

1 tbsp balsamic vinegar

2 red onions

1 bunch thick spring onions

2 shallots

800 g/1¾ lb minced beef (at least 20% fat)

Salt, freshly ground pepper

100 g/½ cup unsalted butter, in small dice,
   plus 1 tbsp

8 slices bacon

4 burger buns

2 mozzarella balls, halved

4 tbsp freshly grated Parmesan cheese

1 head curly lettuce

2 pickled gherkins, sliced

2 tomatoes, sliced

2 tbsp mayonnaise

Basic barbecue sauce (see page 206)

I often stock up on grilled onions
and freeze them. I put 10–20
onions on the barbecue if there are
still embers that have no further use.

1. Grill the Spanish onions with indirect heat for 1 hour and 30 minutes at 150°C/300°F until soft, then leave to cool for 30 minutes. Cut off the root and squeeze out the insides of the onions. Then cut into julienne strips and mix with the balsamic vinegar.

2. Peel and cut the red onions into julienne strips. Grill the spring onions over direct heat on all sides until charred. Wrap in a cloth and rest for 30 minutes. Peel off the charred skin. The peeled spring onions should be soft with a slightly sweet flavour.

3. Peel and finely dice the shallots. Season the mince with salt and pepper. Mix well with 100 g/½ cup of butter and the shallots. Shape the mixture into four burgers with a diameter a little larger than that of the buns.

4. Cook the burgers medium-rare on the cast-iron griddle plate for 2–3 minutes each side. Fry the bacon and red onions in the fat left on the griddle plate. When brown, add 1 tablespoon of butter and leave to melt.

5. Cover the bottom half of the buns with red onions and lay a burger on each. Arrange the bacon slices and spring onions in the form of a cross over the burger. Then top with half a mozzarella ball, 1 tablespoon of Parmesan and 1–2 tablespoons of the balsamic onions and cover with the top half of the bun.

6. Carefully put the burger into a greased sandwich toaster, close the sides and toast for about 15 minutes with indirect heat at 150°C/300°F. Carefully open the sandwich toaster and serve the burger with lettuce, pickled gherkins, tomato slices, mayonnaise and barbecue sauce.

PORTOBELLO SANDWICH

SERVES 4 AS A STARTER
READY IN: 45 MINUTES
DIFFICULTY: ✪✪✪

1 head fresh garlic

3 tbsp unsalted butter

6 tbsp soy sauce

1 tsp mustard

8 Portobello mushrooms

1 fennel bulb

Salt, freshly ground pepper

2 tomatoes

4 slices cheese (such as mozzarella or
  Jarlsberg each about 1-cm/½-in-thick)

2 tbsp white wine vinegar

3 tbsp olive oil

2 red onions

4 slices country-style brown (rye) bread

100 g/2½ cups lamb's lettuce

1. Grill the garlic with indirect heat for about 30 minutes. Warm up the butter in a bowl, then add the soy sauce and mustard and mix well.

2. Break the stems off the mushrooms and lay the caps with the underside facing upwards on the barbecue and fill each one with 1 tablespoon of the butter mixture. Cook the mushrooms with indirect heat for 15 minutes on the grid, heated to about 150°C/300°F, so that the butter can soak in.

3. Using a mandoline slicer finely shave the fennel. Season with salt and pepper. Slice a tomato. Lay one tomato slice and a piece of the cheese inside four of the mushroom caps and cover with fennel. Cover each with a second mushroom cap and put into a greased sandwich toaster.

4. Cook the stuffed mushrooms over a direct heat at 150°C/300°F, then turn and continue to cook for 10 more minutes.

5. In the meantime, mix the vinegar with the oil. Peel the red onions. Use a mandoline slicer to finely shave and add to the mixture. Season with a little salt and pepper. Lightly toast the bread. Halve the second tomato and rub the halves over the toasted bread.

6. Take the garlic off the barbecue and cut off the bottom. Squeeze the soft cloves out of their skin and spread them evenly over the bread. Cover with the lamb's lettuce and arrange the mushrooms on the bread. Drizzle the onion vinaigrette over everything and serve.

MINI BURGER
BUNS

MAKES 12 (BUNS)
READY IN: 1 HOUR 15 MINUTES
DIFFICULTY: ✪✪✪

150 ml/²/₃ cup whole milk

50 g/¼ cup unsalted butter

1 tbsp sugar

1 tsp salt

25 g/1 oz fresh yeast

300 g/2¾ cups plain (all-purpose) flour,
   plus extra for dusting

1 medium egg, beaten

ACCESSORIES
4 x 5-cm/2-in ring moulds

1. Lightly heat the milk (to no higher than 40°C/104°F). Transfer to a food processor and mix with the butter and sugar. Add the salt, yeast and half the flour and work for 8–10 minutes. Gradually add the remaining flour and the egg.

2. Dust the work surface with flour, turn out the dough and shape into twelve small balls. Put the dough balls into ring moulds and prove for 45 minutes.

3. Lay the buns on a baking tray lined with baking parchment and bake with indirect heat inside the barbecue or in a pre-heated oven at 180°C/350°F/Gas 4 for 10–12 minutes. Then make cheese, salmon or pork belly mini burgers (see the following pages).

I'm a big fan of mini burgers because they allow you to try out lots of varieties. Try making these mini burgers and impress your guests with the range of your burger-making skills.

MINI CHEESEBURGER

MAKES 4
READY IN: 20 MINUTES
DIFFICULTY: ✪ ✪ ✪

400 g/14 oz minced beef (at least 20% fat)
4 mini burger buns (see page 65)
4 slices provolone cheese
2 tbsp mayonnaise or burger sauce
2 tbsp basic barbecue sauce (see page 206)
2 pickled gherkins (optional)
1 medium tomato (optional)

1. Make the mince into four small burgers a little larger than the buns. Directly cook over a medium heat, preferably on a cast-iron griddle plate, turning over twice.

2. Cut the buns across the middle and toast the cut side on the barbecue. Lay the cheese slices on the burgers and leave to melt.

3. Spread the buns with mayonnaise or burger sauce, add the burgers and drizzle with barbecue sauce. Optionally, garnish with pickles and tomato.

MINI SALMON BURGER

MAKES 4
READY IN: 30 MINUTES
DIFFICULTY: ✪ ✪ ✪

4 salmon pieces, without skin
   (1–2-cm/½–¾-in-thick) belly or fillet
Salt
4 mini burger buns (see page 65)
1 tbsp unsalted butter
1 tbsp honey
2 tbsp mustard
1 tsp freshly chopped dill
1 lemon
4 tbsp cream cheese
1 tsp horseradish
1 apple, cut into batons
50 g/1¼ cups baby Swiss chard or
   spinach leaves

1. Lightly salt the salmon pieces and trim into a suitable size for the buns. Cut the buns across the middle. Toast the cut side on the barbecue and spread with butter. Mix the honey with the mustard and dill.

2. Directly cook the salmon pieces for 2 minutes on each side over a medium heat on a cast-iron griddle plate, taking care when turning. Halve the lemon and directly cook the halves cut side down on the barbecue for 10 minutes. Then squeeze the juice.

3. Mix the cream cheese with the horseradish, lemon juice and apple batons, and then spread over the bun halves. Place the salmon pieces on the buns, add a little of the honey and mustard sauce and top with a few chard or spinach leaves. Cover with the top half of the buns.

MINI PORK BELLY BURGER

MAKES 4
READY IN: 45 MINUTES
DIFFICULTY: ✪ ✪ ✪

4 mini burger buns (see page 65)
2 onions
Salt
3 tbsp olive oil
4 slices cooked pork belly (2 cm/¾ in thick), or cooked pork sausages
2 tbsp sweet mustard

1. Cut the buns across the middle and toast the cut side on the barbecue.

2. Peel and cut the onions into 1-cm/½-in-thick slices. Season with a little salt and coat with olive oil. Cut the meat to the size of the buns and cook with the onions on a cast-iron griddle plate until brown.

3. Spread the cut sides of the buns with the mustard, cover the bottom half of each with the onions and meat and close with the top half.

MINI MUSHROOM BURGER

MAKES 4
READY IN: 30 MINUTES
DIFFICULTY: ✪ ✪ ✪

8 medium brown mushrooms
2 tbsp basic barbecue sauce (see page 206)
2 tbsp soy sauce
2 green tomatoes
1 red tomato
4 Mini Babybels (cheese)

1. Break the stems off the mushrooms. Mix the barbecue sauce with the soy sauce and coat the undersides of the mushroom caps. Lay the caps with the underside facing upwards on the barbecue and cook for 15 minutes over a medium heat until soft, turning over once.

2. Slice the tomatoes and grill on both sides.

3. Transfer the mushrooms to the indirect cooking side, lay one cheese on each and cook at about 180°C/350°F for about 5 minutes until the cheese begins to melt. Take the mushrooms off the barbecue, cover with tomato slices and complete the burger with another mushroom.

PORK

Pork and pork products are many peoples' favourite barbecue food, whether in the form of sausages, ribs or pork bellies. Pork is cheap and readily available and there is now a growing fan base that extends beyond shoulder steaks and sausages. More and more often, speciality pork cuts such as pork skirt and shoulder eye, which some butchers have never even heard of, are finding their way onto barbecues. Thanks to the internet, television and the increasing number of barbecuing courses, many people are discovering and getting a taste for what gets put on the barbecue in other countries. Thanks to the active barbecuing scene, pulled pork has currently become very popular and is a fixture at any festival and is now offered as a convenience food. This book also makes good use of pork shoulder, but in unusual cuts or in innovative combinations.

SKIRT

DRY-AGED

SHOULDER

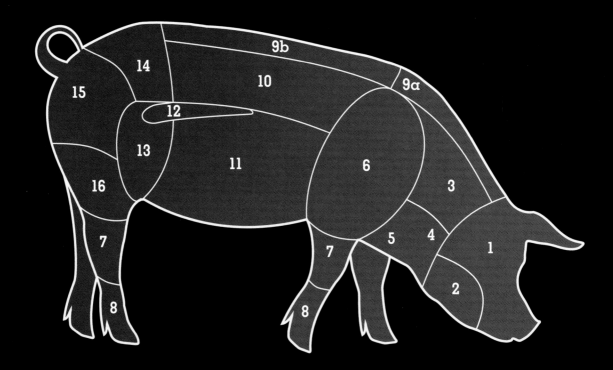

1 Head
2 Cheek
3 Shoulder
4 Breast tip
5 Breast tip
6 Shoulder/blade
7 Knuckle/hock
8 Trotter
9α Neck fat

9b Back fat
10 Loin/chops/skirt
11 Belly
12 Fillet
13 Thick flank
14 Chump
15 Topside/leg
16 Silverside/leg

OUR FAVOURITE MEAT

Pigs are the world's leading source of meat. In terms of numbers, there are more cattle than pigs; however, as pigs are slaughtered at a younger age and reproduce more frequently, five times more pigs than cattle are slaughtered. Moreover, unlike beef, pork doesn't need weeks of ageing. Not more than 48 hours are needed for pork to be ready for consumption. In order to meet consumer demand for cheap and lean meat, the intensive farming of overbred hybrid pigs has become prevalent in recent decades. The meat should be pink, tender and fine-grained, and so animals are largely slaughtered at the age of six to eight months. It's obvious that at such a young age, the animals haven't developed intramuscular fat, and their flavour and texture aren't very pronounced. Fortunately, the market for flavoursome pork with a high proportion of intramuscular fat has been developing for several years now. The healthy, pinkish colour of the meat reveals whether the animal was given much exercise. If it is the colour of an old tea towel, the animal isn't likely to have moved much. A number of breeders are turning to old, robust and stress-free pig breeds, allowing some animals to at least live to see their first birthday, and with less susceptibility to disease.

The popularity of pork for barbecuing is at the very least due to the fact that the different parts can be used and are enhanced by this form of cooking – from whole suckling pigs to the different cuts of animals at slaughtering age, by way of spit-roasted legs and shoulders. As a result, depending on the thickness of the piece, pork shoulder and loin cuts can either be seared on a hot grill or slow cooked at low temperature in the barbecue. Pork shoulder, from which the popular pulled pork is made today, is a part traditionally used for slow cooking at a temperature of up to 120°C/250°F, for example in a water smoker.

FLAVOUR

The flavour of pork is a little sweeter than that of beef. Grilled or roasted pork has a very attractive combination of wood and barnyard flavours, which can be emphasised with mushrooms, garlic, cabbage, potatoes and herbs such as rosemary, sage and thyme, or toned down with sour ingredients such as apple. The savoury flavour of the meat can be brought out with the use of fennel, anise and caramelised onions.

And one mustn't overlook the all-rounder for any barbecue, bacon. There's a saying that goes: 'Everything tastes better if it is wrapped in bacon and grilled.' However there's no need to overdo things with the excessive use of bacon. The discreet use of barding – wrapping in bacon – now and then to keep the inside moist and to give food a slightly salt flavour of the fat is something worth considering.

MONEY MUSCLE
COOKED SOUS-VIDE

SERVES 4 AS A STARTER
SOUS-VIDE COOKING: 24 HOURS
READY IN: 20 MINUTES
DIFFICULTY: ● ● ○

1 pork shoulder
1 tbsp clarified butter
1 tbsp barbecue seasoning (e.g. basic spice rub on page 211)
3 tbsp basic barbecue sauce (see page 206)

EQUIPMENT
Sous-vide machine

1. The previous day, cut out the 'money muscle', part of the neck muscle found on the pork shoulder. It should weigh 200–300 g/7–11 oz. Lightly warm the clarified butter and mix with the barbecue seasoning. Coat the meat with the mixture, vacuum seal in a bag and cook sous-vide for 24 hours at 60°C/140°F.

2. Take the meat out of the bag and pat dry. Transfer to the indirect cooking side of the barbecue heated to 150°C /300°F and cook for 15 minutes, basting repeatedly with the barbecue sauce to glaze. Cut into thin slices and serve.

Money muscle is an American term. At barbecuing competitions, participants are given a cut of pork known as Boston butt, taken from the neck end of the pork shoulder. This cut has to be cooked whole in the competition, and then carved up for the judges as pulled pork and the money muscle. The goal is to impress the judges and increase the likelihood of taking home the prize money. You can buy a pork shoulder and cut it out yourself. It sits at the neck end of the shoulder, above the backbone, and measures 15–20-cm/6–8-in long and 7–10-cm/2¾–4-in wide. The muscle fibres appear to be divided into individual segments.

PULLED PORK
RICE WAFFLE

SERVES 4 AS A STARTER
READY IN: 30 MINUTES
DIFFICULTY: ⚙⚙⚙

200 g/7 oz ready-made pulled pork, flavoured with barbecue sauce (see page 206)

200 g/1 cup steamed rice, sticky if possible

Spray oil

Sweetheart cabbage salad (see page 215), to garnish

2 tbsp basic barbecue sauce (see page 206), as a condiment

1. Mix the pulled pork with the rice to form a sort of dough.

2. Grease a waffle iron with spray oil. Fill the waffle iron with the dough and cook with indirect heat for about 15 minutes at 180°C/350°F.

3. Carefully open the waffle iron, turn out the pulled pork and rice waffle onto a plate and garnish with sweetheart cabbage salad. Repeat the process to make the remaining rice waffles and serve with barbecue sauce.

TOP: Meat Waffle Sandwich
MIDDLE: Noodle Waffle
BOTTOM: Pulled Pork Rice Waffle

With recipes using the waffle iron (also see the following pages) you can use up any leftovers to mix into the basic mixture.

NOODLE
WAFFLE

SERVES 4 FOR BRUNCH
READY IN: 30 MINUTES
DIFFICULTY: ✪ ✪ ✪

2 shallots
1 tbsp olive oil
200 g/7 oz mixed minced meat
Salt, freshly ground pepper
400 g/2¾ cups cooked spaghetti
2 eggs
1 tomato
Spray oil

1. Peel and finely slice the shallots and lightly sauté with the olive oil in a cast-iron frying pan. Season the mince with salt and pepper and add to the pan, pressing on any larger clumps to form small crumbs. Cook until brown.

2. Put the spaghetti into a bowl, add the eggs and season with salt and pepper. Halve the tomato and scoop out the seeds and discard. Dice the flesh.

3. Add the diced tomato and slightly cooled mince to the spaghetti and carefully mix together.

4. Grease a waffle iron well, fill with some of the noodle mixture and cook with indirect heat at 180°C/350°F for about 15 minutes. Carefully open the waffle iron and turn out the waffle onto a plate. Repeat the process to make the remaining waffles. They can be served with a salad.

MEAT WAFFLE SANDWICH

SERVES 4 AS A MAIN COURSE
READY IN: 30 MINUTES
DIFFICULTY: ✪ ✪ ✪

800 g/1¾ lb mixed minced meat

2 tbsp barbecue seasoning (e.g. basic spice rub on page 211)

1 tsp mustard

8 slices toasting bread

Spray oil

FOR THE FILLING

Basic barbecue sauce (see page 206)

Mayonnaise

Sliced pickled gherkins, sliced tomatoes, sliced onions

1. Mix the mince well with the barbecue seasoning and mustard. Put a quarter of the mixture into a greased waffle iron and cook with indirect heat at 150°C/300°F. Repeat the process to make four meat waffles.

2. Take the waffles out of the waffle iron with care. Then place two slices of bread in the waffle iron and toast with indirect heat for 4 minutes. Repeat the process to toast the remaining slices. In the meantime, brush the meat waffles with barbecue sauce and glaze with indirect heat. Make sandwiches with the meat, toast and fillings.

DRY-AGED
PORK CHOP

SERVES 4 AS A MAIN COURSE
READY IN: 45 MINUTES
DIFFICULTY: ✪✪○

2 dry-aged boneless pork chops, skin on
1 tbsp fermented black pepper

FOR THE GINGER CARROTS
8 carrots
½ tsp freshly grated ginger
1 tbsp sweet chilli sauce
1 tsp lemon juice
1 pinch salt
1 tbsp olive oil

1. Remove the skin from the meat and score the fat side of the chops with a close cross-hatch pattern. Stand the chops upright over the scored side on a cold cast-iron griddle plate. Place over a direct heat and slowly heat so that the fat melts and a crust forms. Now cook the meat on the grid for 5–6 minutes, turning over several times, until the internal temperature reaches 58°C/136°F. Cut the chops into thin slices, leaving a little of the fat on each piece.

2. For the ginger carrots, peel the carrots, then use the vegetable peeler to cut into thin strips. Combine with the remaining ingredients on the griddle with the melted fat from the chops. Cook for 10 minutes, stirring regularly.

3. Transfer the vegetables to a plate, arrange the meat strips over the top and season with the pepper.

A dry-aged chop is a very aromatic cut of pork. The pepper fermented with sea salt used for this dish is succulent. The essential oils it contains spark fireworks on the tongue. It provides a wonderful final flourish for fish, steaks and anything you would serve with pepper.

SPARE RIBS

SERVES 4 AS A MAIN COURSE
MARINATING TIME: 12 HOURS
READY IN: 4 HOURS
DIFFICULTY: ✪ ✪ ✪

1 papaya
250 ml/1 cup chicken stock
2 tsp salt
2 tsp sugar
1 tsp cayenne pepper
1 kg/2¼ lb pork spare ribs
5 tbsp clarified butter
3 tbsp barbecue seasoning (e.g. basic
   spice rub on page 211)
100 ml/scant ½ cup apple juice
Basic barbecue sauce (see page 206)

1. Peel the papaya, cut open and scoop out the seeds. Cut the peel into small pieces and set aside with the seeds. Cut the flesh into small dice and put into a bowl. Add the stock, salt, sugar and cayenne pepper, and blend to a purée. Then mix in the papaya peel and seeds, as these contain the highest concentration of papain enzymes.

2. Coat the spare ribs with a generous amount of the marinade and put into a bowl. Cover with cling film and leave to marinate in the refrigerator overnight.

3. Transfer the ribs to a sieve and drain, collecting the marinade. Heat the clarified butter to soften, mix with the barbecue seasoning and rub over the ribs. Mix the apple juice with the collected marinade. Cook the ribs with indirect heat for 1 hour at 130°C/266°F, attaching a smoking tube if available.

4. Transfer the ribs from the barbecue to a sheet of aluminium foil. Cover with the apple juice and marinade mixture and seal the foil to make a pouch. Return the meat in the foil pouch to the barbecue and cook with indirect heat at 130°C/266°F for 2 more hours.

5. Then take the ribs out of the pouch and finally cook for 30 more minutes at 160°C/325°F with indirect heat. Baste the ribs regularly with barbecue sauce in this time to glaze.

I have a feeling that this barbecue classic has over the years developed into as many variants as pigs have bones. The papaya used in the marinade contains the protein-splitting enzyme papain, which acts as a meat tenderiser.

PORK SKIRT WITH
CELERIAC MASH

SERVES 4 AS A MAIN COURSE
READY IN: 1 HOUR
DIFFICULTY: ✪✪○

FOR THE CELERIAC MASH

2 small celeriac
Salt, freshly ground pepper
4 tbsp olive oil
100 ml/scant ½ cup hot milk
4 tbsp unsalted butter

1 kg/2¼ lb pork skirt
Salt
Lemon pepper seasoning

FOR THE MANCHEGO CHEESE
AND TOMATO SAUCE

2 ripe tomatoes
Fleur de sel
Freshly ground pepper
3 tbsp olive oil
3 walnuts
200 g/2 cups Manchego cheese, cubed
1 tbsp fresh rosemary leaves
Rosemary sprigs, to garnish (optional)

1. For the mash, peel and dice the celeriac and spread evenly inside a flame-proof dish. Season with salt and pepper, and drizzle with the oil. Cook inside the barbecue at 180°C/350°F for 45 minutes until soft. Then add the hot milk and butter and blend to a creamy purée. Season with salt and pepper and keep warm.

2. Lightly salt the meat on both sides and set aside for 15 minutes. Then cook on the barbecue over a direct heat at about 180°C/350°F, turning over several times, until the internal temperature reaches 60°C/140°F.

3. In the meantime, make the Manchego cheese and tomato sauce. Halve the tomatoes and coarsely grate into a bowl. Season with salt and pepper, and mix in the oil. Crack the walnuts, crush the kernels with your hands and add to the tomatoes. Add the cheese cubes. Coarsely chop the rosemary leaves, add to the bowl and mix everything well.

4. Take the meat off the barbecue and cut against the grain into 1-cm/½-in-thick slices. Sprinkle with a little lemon pepper and serve on four plates with the sauce and celeriac mash. Optionally, garnish with sprigs of rosemary.

TACOS

SERVES 6 AS A MAIN COURSE
MARINATING TIME: 1–2 HOURS
READY IN: 1 HOUR
DIFFICULTY: ✪✪○

1–1.5 kg/2¼–3¼ lb pork shoulder
Salt
1 pineapple
2 Spanish onions
6 (18-cm/7-in-diameter) tortillas
200 g/scant 1 cup sour cream
1 bunch coriander, finely chopped
1 lime

FOR THE MARINADE

1 tbsp sriracha (hot chilli) sauce
1 tbsp garlic paste
1 tbsp ginger paste
2 tbsp soy sauce
Juice 1 lime
100 ml/scant ½ cup sparkling mineral
   water
Salt, freshly ground pepper

1. Cut the pork shoulder into 5-cm/2½-in cubes and lightly season with salt. Mix together the ingredients for the marinade. Peel and cut the pineapple into 2-cm/¾-in-thick slices, then trim and cut the slices into smaller pieces. Set aside. Add the trimmings and core pieces to the marinade. Mix in the meat and marinate in the refrigerator for 1–2 hours.

2. Peel and quarter the onions and separate three of the quarters into three-layer-thick segments. Cut the remaining quarter into julienne strips. Set aside. Pat the meat dry and thread onto metal skewers, alternating with the pineapple and onion segments. Position the skewers on the barbecue, keeping the meat from having direct contact with the grid. I recommend using 6 prongs of a rotisserie kit. Cook the meat for 45–60 minutes at 150–170°C/300–340°F until it is soft enough to be easily pulled off the skewer, basting once or twice with the marinade.

3. Spread the tortillas with sour cream. Take the meat off the skewers and cut into small pieces together with the onions and pineapple. Add to the tortillas. Top with the julienned onion, coriander and drizzle with a little lime juice, and roll up the tortillas.

PORK BELLY

SERVES 6 AS A MAIN COURSE
MARINATING TIME: 12–24 HOURS
+ 8 HOURS RESTING TIME
READY IN: 3 HOURS
DIFFICULTY: ✪✪○

4 tbsp salt
4 tbsp sugar
2 tsp freshly ground pepper
1 kg/2¼ lb pork belly

1. Mix the salt with the sugar and pepper. Rub the pork belly well with the mixture and put into a freezer bag. Leave to marinate in the refrigerator for 12–24 hours.

2. Transfer the pork belly to an aluminium container and cook with indirect heat for 30 minutes at 230°C/450°F, then lower the temperature to 130°C/266°F. Cook the meat for 1 hour 30 minutes more, until its internal temperature reaches 65°C/149°F, then take it off the barbecue and leave to cool. Wrap the meat in aluminium foil and refrigerate for 8 hours.

3. Take the cold pork belly out of the refrigerator, cut into slices and grill on a cast-iron griddle plate until brown and crispy.

PORK SHOULDER
WITH GRILLED LEEKS

SERVES 6 AS A MAIN COURSE
READY IN: 45 MINUTES
DIFFICULTY: ✪ ✪ ✪

About 700 g/1 lb 9 oz boned pork
    shoulder
Salt, freshly ground pepper
Sweet paprika and demerara sugar, or
    barbecue seasoning (e.g. basic spice
    rub on page 211)
6 thick leeks

FOR THE SAUCE

1 tbsp white wine vinegar
4 tbsp peanut oil
2 tsp mustard
Salt, freshly ground pepper

1. Rub the meat all over with a mixture of salt and pepper with a pinch of paprika and demerara sugar, or with barbecue seasoning. Cook over indirect heat for 30–40 minutes at about 180°C/350°F until the internal temperature of the meat reaches about 58°C/136°F.

2. In the meantime, cut off the green part of the leeks and discard. Leave the roots attached; they will char on the barbecue and give a pleasant smoky aroma. Cook the leeks over a direct heat, turning over regularly (three or four times) until they are soft. They can be allowed to turn black on the outside.

3. Mix together the ingredients for the sauce and season with salt and pepper.

4. Take the leeks off the barbecue and cut off 2 cm/¾ in from the top and bottom of each stalk. Use a finger from the root end to push the tender inside of the leeks out of the charred exterior.

5. Put a leek onto each of six plates and drizzle with sauce. Slice up the meat, arrange over the leek and season with a pinch of salt and pepper.

PORK SHOULDER
BURRITO

SERVES 6 AS A MAIN COURSE
READY IN: 1 HOUR
DIFFICULTY: ✪✪✪

1.5 kg/3¼ lb pork shoulder
Salt and freshly ground pepper, or
    Brazilian barbecue seasoning or basic
    spice rub (see page 211)
Basic barbecue sauce (see page 206)
6 (18-cm/7-in-diameter) tortillas

FOR THE FILLING
½ head red cabbage
1 tbsp salt
1 chilli pepper
Juice ½ lime
2 tbsp sugar
1 red onion
1 bunch coriander
200 g/scant 1 cup sour cream
2 tbsp sesame seeds

1. Cut the shoulder lengthways into six strips of equal size. Season with salt and pepper, or with the Brazilian barbecue seasoning or basic spice rub and thread onto skewers.

2. Hang the skewers from the barbecue warming rack, or alternatively, stand them between the bars of the grid and cook the meat for 30 minutes at about 180°C/350°F, then reduce the temperature to 120°C/250°F and cook for 30 more minutes until tender. As they cook, baste the skewers with barbecue sauce three times, turning over each time.

3. In the meantime, use a mandoline slicer to shave the cabbage, mix with the salt and leave to stand for 20 minutes. Finely chop the chilli pepper and mix with the cabbage. Add the lime juice and sugar and season with salt. Peel the onion and slice into rings. Finely chop the coriander.

4. Heat both sides of the tortillas quickly on the barbecue to soften and infuse with toasted flavours. Spread each with 2 tablespoons of sour cream. Cover the tortilla with red cabbage and add the meat from one skewer. Scatter with onion rings, coriander and a sprinkling of sesame seeds, and roll up the tortillas. To serve, wrap the burritos in aluminium foil, or cut them into bite-sized pieces.

LEG OF SUCKLING PIG WITH WATERMELON

SERVES 4 AS A MAIN COURSE
READY IN: 1 HOUR 30 MINUTES
DIFFICULTY: ✪ ✪ ✪

1 leg of suckling pig
Salt, freshly ground pepper
½ watermelon
4 tbsp olive oil
1 tbsp finely chopped rosemary leaves
1 lemon

FOR THE MARINADE
100 ml/scant ½ cup apple juice
100 ml/scant ½ cup meat stock
2 dashes Tabasco sauce

1. Use a sharp knife to score the skin of the leg with lines about 1 cm/½ in apart to form a cross-hatch pattern. Mix together the ingredients for the marinade and inject the marinade into the leg using a marinade injector. Season the outside of the leg with salt and pepper and cook with indirect heat at 120°C/250°F for 1 hour until the internal temperature reaches 60°C/140°F.

2. In the meantime, cut off the skin from the watermelon and cut into 2-cm/¾-in-thick slices, removing as many of the seeds as possible. Drizzle the watermelon with the olive oil and season with rosemary, salt and pepper. Grill for 5 minutes on each side. Quarter the lemon and put onto the barbecue to warm the juice.

3. Take the meat off the barbecue and set aside in a warm place. Heat the barbecue to the highest temperature and sear for 5 minutes to turn the skin crispy. Alternatively, a heat gun can be applied to the skin.

4. Divide the watermelon onto four plates and drizzle with a little warm lemon juice. Cut up the meat and arrange over the watermelon.

BACON-WRAPPED BANANA

SERVES 6 AS A SNACK
READY IN: 20 MINUTES
DIFFICULTY: ✪ ✪ ✪

2 bananas
2 tbsp soy sauce
2 slices streaky bacon
1 tbsp ginger paste
Freshly ground pepper
1 red onion
Salt
1 tbsp red wine vinegar
1 tbsp olive oil

1. Peel the bananas and brush with soy sauce.

2. Lay the bacon slices on a chopping board and smooth with a knife to make longer and thinner. This will turn them crispy when cooked. Spread the bacon slices with ginger paste and season with pepper, then wrap one tightly around each banana. Cook with indirect heat for 15 minutes at 180°C/350°F until the bacon turns crispy.

3. In the meantime, slice the onion very finely – I only use the outer layers because the flavour of the inner layers is too intense. Mix the onion with a pinch of salt, the vinegar and oil.

4. Cut the bananas into bite-sized pieces and sprinkle with the seasoned onion.

ONIONS WITH BACON

SERVES 6 AS A SNACK
READY IN: 1 HOUR 30 MINUTES
DIFFICULTY ✪ ✪ ✪

6 Spanish onions
100 g/½ cup bacon, diced
100 g/1 cup Cheddar cheese, grated
120 g/½ cup sour cream
Freshly ground pepper
Basil leaves, finely chopped

1. Peel the onions and make several incisions across the top. Do not cut too deeply, otherwise the onion will fall apart. Fill the incisions with bacon.

2. Cook the onions with indirect heat for 1 hour at 150°C/300°F, preferably on a cast-iron griddle plate. They should be soft enough to be able to press flat with a wide spoon.

3. Sprinkle grated cheese over the onions and cook for 15 minutes more to melt the cheese. Finally, top with a little sour cream and sprinkle with a little pepper and basil.

LOIN OF SUCKLING PIG WITH TUNA SAUCE

SERVES 4 AS A MAIN COURSE
READY IN: 30 MINUTES
DIFFICULTY: ✪✪✪

1 suckling pig loin, boned
Salt
200 g/5 cups baby spinach
5 sprigs thyme
Freshly ground pepper

FOR THE SAUCE
100 g/½ cup tinned tuna
2 medium eggs
3 tbsp milk
200 ml/scant 1 cup olive oil
2 tbsp lemon juice
3 anchovy fillets
2 tbsp capers

1. Combine all the ingredients for the sauce in a blender and purée.

2. Remove the skin from the meat and score the remaining fat with a close cross-hatch pattern. Lightly season the meat with salt and place fat-side down on a cold cast-iron griddle plate.

3. Gradually heat the griddle on the barbecue for 20 minutes to melt the fat and form a nice crust. Then transfer the meat to the grid over a direct high heat and sear, turning over several times to develop toasted flavours. When the internal temperature of the meat reaches 60°C/140°F, take off the barbecue and set aside in a warm place.

4. Wilt the spinach in the fat on the griddle. Season with salt and pepper. Cut the meat into 2–3-cm/¾–1¼-in-thick slices.

5. Divide up the spinach between four plates and arrange the meat on top. Cover with the tuna sauce and garnish with thyme leaves.

The loin can also be cooked on a rotisserie (see photo). In this case, season the boned loin with salt and roll up. Tie the roll with twine and skewer through the middle with the rotisserie rod and secure. Roast at 150°C/300°F for about 45 minutes until the internal temperature reaches 60°C/140°F. Then raise the temperature to 180°C/350°F and continue to cook until a nice crust forms.

TOAST HAWAII

SERVES 4 AS A MAIN COURSE
MARINATING TIME: 4 HOURS
READY IN: 30 MINUTES
DIFFICULTY: ✪✪✪

---

2 pork shoulder steaks (3-cm/1¼-in-thick)
6 slices bacon
4 slices toasting bread
2 cloves garlic, halved
4 slices pineapple
4 cocktail cherries
4 slices Gouda cheese

FOR THE MARINADE
½ tsp salt
1 pinch mustard
1 Spanish onion, sliced
300 ml/1¼ cups beer
2 tbsp mustard
3 dashes Tabasco sauce

1. Mix together the ingredients for the marinade and marinate the steaks for 4 hours.

2. Take the steaks out of the marinade, pat dry and cook with indirect heat for about 30 minutes until the internal temperature reaches 60°C/140°F. Finally, sear for 3 minutes over a direct heat until the steaks are browned and crispy.

3. While the steaks are cooking, grill the bacon until crispy, then pat dry with kitchen paper. Lightly toast one side of the bread directly over one side of the grid. Rub the toasted side with the garlic.

4. Cut the steaks into strips and arrange on the toast. Crumble the bacon over the meat. Top with a slice of pineapple, pop a cherry in the hole of the pineapple and finish with cheese slices.

5. Turn up the heat and apply indirect heat until the cheese melts. Alternatively, if you like, you can improvise a charcoal salamander grill, as shown in the image.

BLOODY HARRY

SERVES 4 AS A STARTER
READY IN: 30 MINUTES
DIFFICULTY: ✪✪✪

2 red onions
1 tomato
8 slices black pudding
1–2 tbsp flour
12 slices firm apple
12 round slices pumpernickel
2 tbsp olive oil
1 tbsp white wine vinegar
Salt, freshly ground pepper

FOR THE SAUCE

250 ml/1 cup ketchup
4 tbsp freshly grated horseradish
1 tbsp soy sauce
Juice of ½ lime
1 dash Tabasco sauce, salt

1. Peel the onions and cut into eight slices the same size as the apple slices. Cut the tomato into 5-mm/¼-in-thick slices.

2. Heat a cast-iron griddle pan. Sprinkle the black pudding with flour and cook on both sides until lightly crisp. Grill both sides of the onion, apple and pumpernickel slices on the griddle, allowing the bread to soak up the fat released by the black pudding.

3. In the meantime, mix together the ingredients for the sauce. Cut the trimmings from the apple, tomato and onions, together with a little bread, into thin strips, drizzle with the olive oil and vinegar, and season with salt and pepper. Make a bed with the mixture on four plates.

4. Make four towers on the plates by stacking the grilled slices in the following order: bread, apple, pudding, onion, tomato, bread, apple, pudding, onion, bread. Secure each tower with a skewer and pour over 2 tablespoons of sauce.

BLACK PUDDING AND RHUBARB
SANDWICH

SERVES 4 AS A STARTER
READY IN: 30 MINUTES
DIFFICULTY: ✪✪✪

3 shallots
1 tsp olive oil
3 thin sticks rhubarb
1 tbsp red wine vinegar
1 tsp sugar beet syrup
Salt, freshly ground pepper
200 g/7 oz black pudding
2 slices toasting bread
4 sprigs thyme

1. Peel and finely dice the shallots and fry in the olive oil on a hot plancha (smooth) griddle plate. Clean the rhubarb sticks, cut into 1 cm/½ in lengths and add to the shallots. As soon as the rhubarb is soft, add the vinegar and syrup, and season with salt and pepper.

2. Cut the black pudding into 1-cm/½-in-thick slices and grill on both sides on the griddle.

3. In the meantime, toast the bread and halve across the middle. Top the toast with the rhubarb chutney and pudding, and garnish each serving with a sprig of thyme.

POTATO AND MEATLOAF BURGER

SERVES 4 AS A MAIN COURSE
READY IN: 45 MINUTES
DIFFICULTY: ✪✪✪

FOR THE POTATO CAKES

4 tomatoes
500 g/1¼ lb floury potatoes
100 g/½ cup unsalted butter
1 bunch spring onions
1 bunch parsley
3 tbsp flour

FOR THE BURGER

4 slices meatloaf
1 Spanish onion
4 large lettuce leaves
Sweet mustard
2 pickled gherkins, cut into 16 slices

FOR THE BURGER SAUCE

2 tbsp mayonnaise
1 tbsp sweet chilli sauce
½ tsp mustard
1 tsp ketchup
1 dash Tabasco sauce
1 pinch salt

1. To make the potato cakes, blanch, peel and finely dice the tomatoes, and leave to drain on kitchen paper. Peel the potatoes and boil in salted water until soft. Drain and mash or press through a potato ricer. Melt the butter. Finely chop the spring onions and parsley, and stir into the mashed potatoes together with the tomatoes, flour and melted butter. Shape the mixture into eight balls, flatten and bake in the barbecue with indirect heat at 200°C/400°F for 20 minutes.

2. Trim the slices of meatloaf to the size of the potato cakes and sear on both sides over a direct heat until sear marks develop.

3. Peel the onion and cut into thin rings. Mix all the ingredients for the burger sauce together well.

4. When serving, spread four of the potato cakes with burger sauce. Cover with a lettuce leaf and a few onion rings, add a slice of meatloaf and spread with a generous amount of sweet mustard. Arrange four gherkin slices on top and cover with a second potato cake.

GRILLED ASPARAGUS
WITH EGG SAUCE

SERVES 4 AS A MAIN COURSE
READY IN: 30 MINUTES
DIFFICULTY: ✪✪✪

Salt, sugar

12 white asparagus spears

12 green asparagus spears

12 slices serrano ham

2 eggs, soft-boiled

100 g/½ cup beurre noisette

1 tbsp lemon juice

Freshly ground pepper

2 tbsp fried onions

1. Mix 1 litre of water with 2 tablespoons each of salt and sugar.

2. Wash the unpeeled asparagus spears and soak in the water for 30 minutes. Halve each ham slice lengthways.

3. Drain the asparagus and wrap each of the tips with a strip of ham to protect from the heat. Grill the asparagus on all sides over a direct heat at about 150°C/300°F for 20 minutes until cooked.

4. Blend the eggs with the beurre noisette and lemon juice. Season with salt and pepper.

5. Cut off 1 cm/½ in of the woody end and peel the lower third of the green asparagus spears. Peel the white asparagus spears and cut off the woody ends. Arrange the asparagus on four plates, cover with the sauce and garnish with fried onions.

GAME & LAMB

Barbecued game is an extraordinary experience. Not only wild boar, but also venison and roe deer are excellent when cooked this way. Wild animals live freely in the forest and feed exclusively on what nature provides. Nothing could be more organic. Game is now available in every season from large retailers, butchers and specialist game meat suppliers. Any meat lover would be happy to be served a well-prepared game dish. Presently, only few people associate barbecuing with game, although this should change. In my opinion, this way of cooking game is underestimated because it opens up a range of creative culinary options for a change from the traditional stews. Nowadays, with the possibility of guaranteeing a continuous cold chain, the processing of fresh game meat is no longer a problem. As this was a problem in the past, game meat would be marinated for a long time to cover up the more or less pronounced gamey flavour – the slight flavour of decay also known as *haut gout*. Then the meat would be stewed for hours on end to make it palatable; however, served with plenty of sauce and cranberries, it could also be very delicious.

DUCK

VENISON

LAMB

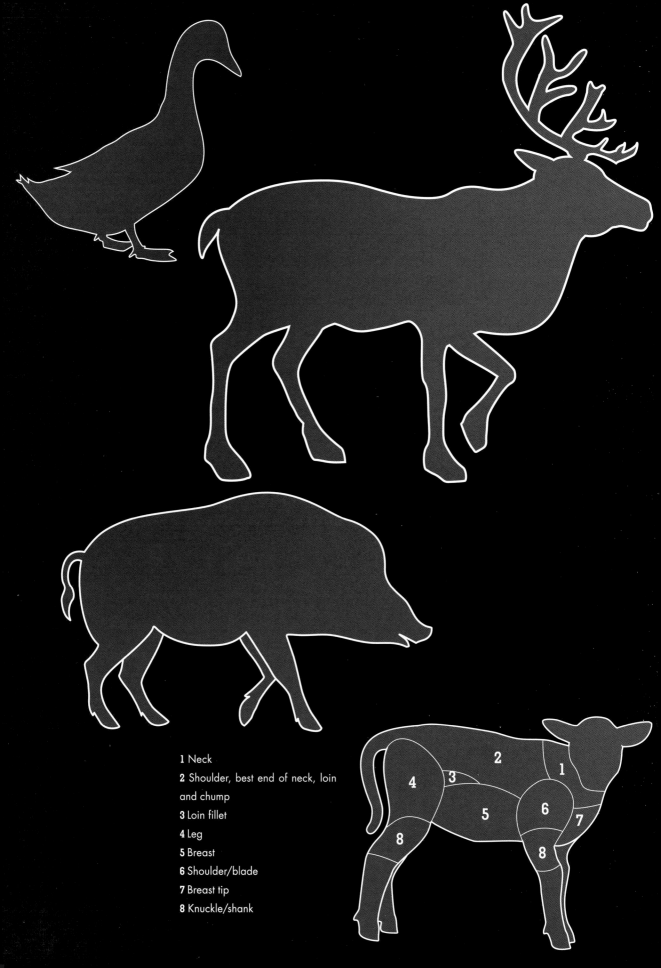

1 Neck

2 Shoulder, best end of neck, loin and chump

3 Loin fillet

4 Leg

5 Breast

6 Shoulder/blade

7 Breast tip

8 Knuckle/shank

UNIQUE FLAVOUR

The flesh of animals such as lamb, local game, duck and quail, I believe, feature too rarely at barbecues, despite their unique flavour.

I often find myself salivating as I research new duck dishes. Then I lean back and try to imagine the delicate, aromatic taste, which also lends itself to combinations with fruity-sweet and savoury flavours. Duck is probably the best compromise for people who find chicken too mundane and goose too strong.

The same thing happens when I'm in the Mediterranean and I see rabbit on a restaurant menu, which I relish. Then I think to myself: 'You should do rabbit more often.' Very seldom is this fine white meat, whether braised or grilled, served anywhere. It is only with the trend for Mediterranean cuisine that long-neglected rabbit is making a well-deserved comeback, and it's becoming increasingly popular.

Lamb, the classic of Mediterranean and Arab cuisine, makes an impressive barbecue. Almost all lamb cuts can be enhanced this way. Particularly suitable are cuts taken from the loin, either as chops or eye of loin, not to mention the loin fillets. Even legs of lamb and the other leg cuts come out beautifully on the barbecue. The range extends to spare ribs of spring lamb and breast of lamb, rolled shoulder roast, spicy lamb sausages, such as merguez, and delicacies made from minced lamb, such as cevapcici and kofta. As a general rule, lamb for barbecuing should be light to dark red colour and not too lean – ideally, it should have fine marbling. Lamb is a winner because of

its subtle and unique flavour and combines wonderfully with Mediterranean spices.

STUFFED HOKKAIDO SQUASH

SERVES 4 AS A MAIN COURSE
READY IN: 1 HOUR 30 MINUTES
DIFFICULTY: ✪✪○

800 g/1¾ lb wild boar neck
Salt
1 hokkaido squash
1 tbsp mustard
1–2 cloves garlic, crushed
1 tsp ground caraway seeds
Freshly ground pepper
200 g/7 oz small potatoes, cooked
1 Spanish onion

1. Cut the meat into 3-cm/1¼-in cubes and lightly season with salt. Cut off the top of the squash to make a lid. Hollow out the squash and lightly season the inside with salt.

2. Brown the meat on all sides over a direct heat on the barbecue. Transfer to a bowl and mix with the mustard and garlic, and season with the caraway, salt and pepper.

3. Halve the potatoes. Peel the onion and roughly chop. Add the potatoes and onion to the meat, mix well and fill the squash. Cover with the lid.

4. Carefully place the squash into an aluminium container (if it becomes too soft, it may fall apart) and cook for 1 hour at 150°C/300°F. Carefully take the squash out of the barbecue and serve. The skin can be eaten.

WILD BOAR
ROLLS

SERVES 4 AS A STARTER
READY IN: 30 MINUTES
DIFFICULTY: ●●○

200 g/7 oz red cabbage
1 pinch sugar
Salt, freshly ground pepper
100 g/½ cup unsalted butter
1 tbsp balsamic vinegar
1 packet filo pastry (from the refrigerated
    section of a supermarket)
200 g/7 oz pulled wild boar (see
    opposite)

1. Use a mandoline slicer to finely shave the cabbage. Season with the sugar, salt and pepper, and knead together thoroughly for at least 3 minutes.

2. Melt 1 tablespoon of butter in a cast-iron frying pan and sauté the cabbage until tender but still a little firm to the bite. Deglaze the pan with the vinegar. Melt in the remaining butter.

3. Lay two sheets of filo pastry, one on top of the other, on the work surface and cut into 10-cm/4-in squares. Mix the pulled wild boar with the cabbage and put 1–2 tablespoons of the mixture on each pastry square, covering half. Brush the edges of the pastry with melted butter and carefully roll up the squares. Seal the edges closed by pressing a little firmly.

4. Bake the rolls on a pre-heated pizza stone for 10–15 minutes, turning over twice, until brown on all sides.

PULLED WILD BOAR

BASIC RECIPE TO SERVE 15
READY IN: ABOUT 20 HOURS
DIFFICULTY: ✪✪✪

3 kg/6½ lb wild boar shoulder or neck
Salt
400 ml/1⅔ cups game stock

FOR THE SEASONING PASTE
200 g/1 cup clarified butter
1 tbsp salt
2 tbsp sweet paprika
2 tbsp salt
1 tbsp brown sugar
1 tbsp mustard

I have consciously held back on adding the typical seasonings used with game meat, so as to allow the flavour of the wild boar to come through. However, feel free to flavour the cooked pulled wild boar with juniper berries, bay leaves, allspice, thyme and rosemary. Because it takes so long to make, I always make more than I need and freeze the meat in serving portions.

1. Pat the meat dry, lightly season all over with salt and leave to stand for 20 minutes.

2. Warm the clarified butter slightly to soften, and then mix with the rest of the seasoning paste ingredients. Rub the meat all over with this paste.

3. Set the barbecue to a maximum temperature of 110°C/230°F. Put the meat into an aluminium container and cook with indirect heat for 3 hours. Occasionally baste the meat with the melted fat inside the container.

4. Then lay the meat directly on the grid and cook for 1 hour. A smoking tube can be attached and the meat smoked at this time.

5. Take the meat off the barbecue and wrap in aluminium foil, together with the stock and the fat from the container. Cook with indirect heat until the internal temperature reaches 90°C/194°F. This can take 12–15 hours.

6. Then turn off the barbecue and leave the meat until the internal temperature falls to 60°C/140°F. Open the foil and transfer the meat to a bowl. Shred the meat, collecting any liquid and mixing it in again.

LOIN OF VENISON
WITH RADICCHIO

SERVES 4 AS A MAIN COURSE
READY IN: 2 HOURS
DIFFICULTY: ✪✪✪

1 kg/2¼ lb venison loin, ready to cook
Salt
100 g/½ cup clarified butter
3 tbsp game herbs and spices (juniper
   berries, allspice, bay leaf, oregano,
   rosemary)

FOR THE RADICCHIO

6 tbsp pumpkin seed oil
2 tbsp balsamic vinegar
2 tbsp sugar beet syrup
Salt, freshly ground pepper
2 heads radicchio

ACCESSORIES

Fir or spruce branches

1. Lightly salt the meat and leave to stand in a warm place for 15 minutes. Warm the clarified butter slightly to soften, and then mix with the herbs and spices. Rub the meat with the resulting paste.

2. Put the fir branches in the indirect cooking side of the barbecue. Lay the meat over them and cook for 1 hour 30 minutes at 150°C/300°F, turning over several times, until the internal temperature reaches 60°C/140°F.

3. In the meantime, mix the oil with the vinegar and syrup, and season with salt and pepper. Halve the heads of radicchio and drizzle the cut side with some of the seasoned oil. Set the rest of the oil aside in a warm place.

4. Put the radicchio halves cut-side down on the hot grid at 180°C/350°F and cook with indirect heat for 15–20 minutes until they have wilted a little. Take them off the barbecue and cut into strips.

5. Put the radicchio into a dish and drizzle with seasoned oil. Slice the meat and arrange over the radicchio.

LEG OF ROE VENISON
WITH ROSEMARY-STUDDED APPLES

SERVES 4 AS A MAIN COURSE
READY IN: 3 HOURS
DIFFICULTY: ✪ ✪ ✪

1–1.5-kg/2¼–3¼ lb leg of roe venison, boned
2 shallots
3 tbsp clarified butter
2 sprigs rosemary
Salt, freshly ground pepper
3 sprigs thyme
1 clove garlic
Grated zest 1 untreated lemon
3 tbsp olive oil

FOR THE ROSEMARY-STUDDED APPLE
1 walnut-sized piece ginger
4 apples (e.g. Belle de Boskop, or other cooking apples)
4 sprigs rosemary

1. Trim the roe deer leg. Peel and finely dice the shallots. Fry the meat trimmings in the clarified butter with a sprig of rosemary and the shallots. This will flavour the clarified butter. Take out the larger pieces and leave to cool.

2. Season the meat all over with salt and pepper. Pluck the leaves from the second spring of rosemary and the thyme. Peel the garlic and crush through a garlic press, Mix with the rosemary and thyme leaves, lemon zest and oil. Mix in the clarified butter.

3. Rub the meat with half the seasoning oil and cook with indirect heat for 1 hour at a maximum temperature of 120°C/250°F. Then baste the meat with the rest of the seasoning oil and continue to cook for 1 hour 30 minutes until the internal temperature reaches 60°C/140°F.

4. In the meantime, make the rosemary-studded apples by peeling the ginger and cutting into batons. Stud the apples with the rosemary sprigs and ginger batons and bake with indirect heat at 120°C/250°F for 30–40 minutes until soft.

5. Cut the meat into slices and arrange on four plates with the baked apples.

LAMB KOFTA
SKEWERS

SERVES 4–6 AS A MAIN COURSE
READY IN: 45 MINUTES
DIFFICULTY: ✪✪✪

1 Spanish onion
2 bunches parsley
1 handful mint leaves
1 handful dill
1.5 kg/3¼ lb minced lamb
1 tbsp coriander seeds, lightly toasted
1 tbsp fennel seeds, lightly toasted
1 tsp smoked paprika
½ tsp cayenne pepper
½ tsp chilli flakes
2½ tsp salt
1 tbsp ground caraway seeds

FOR THE YOGHURT DIP
150 g/⅔ cup set yoghurt
100 g/scant ½ cup smetana (sour cream)
5 tbsp olive oil
1 pinch finely chopped red chilli pepper
1 pinch sugar
Salt
Juice and grated zest 1 untreated lemon

1. Peel, halve and finely grate the onion. Finely chop the parsley, mint and dill and mix with the onion. Put the mince into a bowl and mix with the onion and herb mixture. Crush the coriander and fennel seeds in a mortar. Combine with the remaining spices and sprinkle over the meat. Carefully knead everything together for at least 3 minutes.

2. Put the meat into two 3-litre/5¼ pint freezer bags and mix again in the bags. Cut off one corner of the bag, leaving a 2½–3-cm/1–1¼-in wide opening.

3. Insert a metal skewer into one of the bags through the opening. Press mince around the skewer and take it out. Repeat the process with the seven remaining skewers, using up all the mince.

4. Lay the skewers on the indirect cooking side of the barbecue and cook for 20–30 minutes at about 180°C/350°F, turning over several times. The skewers can be stood between the bars of the grid, leaving the meat free from contact. In the meantime, make the dip by mixing the yoghurt with the smetana in a bowl until smooth. Add the olive oil and season with the chilli, sugar and salt. Finally, flavour with a little lemon juice and zest. Serve the kofta with the dip.

Kofta also make a wonderful filling for wraps. Add onion rings, pepper slices and the yoghurt dip to the tortillas, and then top with the kofta and roll up.

SHOULDER OF LAMB
WITH MANGETOUT

SERVES 4 AS A MAIN COURSE
READY IN: 1 HOUR 15 MINUTES
DIFFICULTY: ✪✪✿

1 lamb shoulder, boned
   (about 1 kg/2¼ lb)
Salt
3 cloves garlic
6 anchovy fillets in oil, drained
Olive oil
200 g/7 oz mangetout
2 sprigs rosemary
Freshly ground pepper
Grated zest 1 untreated lemon

1. Lightly salt the meat on all sides. Use a thin pointed knife to make six small holes. Peel and halve the garlic, and insert one half-clove and one anchovy fillet into each hole.

2. Rub the meat with olive oil and cook with indirect heat for about 1 hour at 120°C/250°F until the internal temperature reaches 58°C/136°F.

3. In the meantime, put the mangetout into a bowl, drizzle lightly with olive oil and mix. Cook on both sides with direct heat (preferably on a barbecue tray) until blisters form in places.

4. Take the meat off the barbecue and set aside in a warm place. Turn up the heat of the barbecue to the highest setting. Return the meat to the barbecue and sear each side for 20 seconds until sear marks develop, If you have a Napoleon barbecue with a Sizzle Zone, you can take the meat straight from the cooking area and immediately sear it there.

5. Finely chop the rosemary leaves and mix with salt, pepper and the lemon zest. Divide up the mangetout between four plates, and then slice and arrange the meat on top. Sprinkle everything with the rosemary seasoning and drizzle with a little olive oil.

RABBIT LOIN
IN A BREAD CRUST

SERVES 4 AS A MAIN COURSE
READY IN: 45 MINUTES
DIFFICULTY: ✪✪✪

2 rabbit loins with belly flap attached,
    rolled and ready to cook
Salt
2 mozzarella balls
4 cherry tomatoes
65 g/¾ cup freshly grated Parmesan
    cheese
Sweet paprika
Olive oil
15 basil leaves
2 slices tramezzini (white, crustless,
    rectangular) bread or 4 slices toasting
    bread, crust removed
6 slices streaky bacon

1. Unroll the loins and lightly season the meat with salt. Finely dice the mozzarella and tomatoes. Add the Parmesan and season the mixture with paprika and a little olive oil. Mix well. Cover the meat with basil leaves and coat with the cheese mixture.

2. Roll out the tramezzini bread slices with a rolling pin to make thinner, then lay on the work surface slightly overlapped. Lay the bacon on the work surface and smooth with a knife to make longer and thinner.

3. Roll up the cheese-coated loins again inside the belly flap, then lay on the bread and roll up tightly. Wrap the rolls in bacon and cook with indirect heat for 30 minutes at 150°C/300°F. Cut each loin in half to serve.

LEG OF RABBIT
WITH SWEET POTATO

SERVES 4 AS A MAIN COURSE
MARINATING TIME: 12 HOURS
READY IN: 1 HOUR 30 MINUTES
DIFFICULTY: ●●○

4 rabbit legs
Salt, freshly ground pepper
100 ml/scant ½ cup white wine
200 ml/scant 1 cup olive oil plus extra for
   the cabbage
14 sprigs thyme
1 dash Tabasco sauce
1 tbsp mustard
2 tbsp teriyaki sauce
4 sweet potatoes
1 lemon
100 g/½ cup unsalted butter
1 Chinese cabbage

1. Season the legs with salt and pepper. Mix the wine, oil, 4 sprigs of thyme, the Tabasco sauce, mustard and teriyaki sauce inside a ziplock bag. Add the legs, seal the bag and marinate in the refrigerator for at least 12 hours.

2. Boil the sweet potatoes in water or cook on the barbecue in an aluminium container at 200°C/400°F for about 1 hour, depending on the size, until soft. In the meantime, halve the lemon and cook directly on the cut side until light golden. Melt the butter in a pan and lightly season with salt. Squeeze the lemon halves into the pan and add the 10 remaining thyme sprigs. Infuse the butter with the thyme for about 30 minutes.

3. Thread the legs onto two skewers (see photo) or simply cook with indirect heat for about 45 minutes at 150°C/300°F. Then cook directly over the heat until sear marks develop.

4. In the meantime, halve the Chinese cabbage, lightly season the cut side with salt and brush with olive oil. Put the cabbage cut-side down on the indirect cooking side of the barbecue and cook for 20 minutes.

5. Lightly press all around the soft sweet potatoes to make small holes. Use a marinade injector to inject the thyme butter into the holes.

6. Halve the Chinese cabbage halves again, and serve each piece on a plate with a rabbit leg and a sweet potato.

QUAIL
WITH WARM ROCKET SALAD

SERVES 4 AS A MAIN COURSE
MARINATING TIME: 2 HOURS
READY IN: 45 MINUTES
DIFFICULTY: ✪✪✪

4 quails
Salt

FOR THE MARINADE

1 clove garlic
5 sprigs thyme
2 sprigs rosemary
½ tsp salt
1 pinch cayenne pepper
3 tbsp olive oil
Grated zest 1 untreated lemon

FOR THE SALAD

100 g/2½ cups rocket
2 red onions
1 bunch radishes
Salt, freshly ground pepper
3 tbsp soy sauce
Juice of 1 lemon

1. For the marinade, peel and finely chop the garlic and pluck the thyme and rosemary leaves. Crush the salt with the cayenne pepper in a mortar, add the olive oil, garlic and herbs and work to a paste. Stir in the lemon zest.

2. Lay the quails on their breasts. Use kitchen shears to cut along both sides of their backbones and remove. Press on the quails to spread out and remove their breastbones.

3. Blanch the quails for 40 seconds in boiling water, refresh in iced water for 2 minutes and carefully pat dry. Lightly salt the meat and leave to stand for 10 minutes. Rub the quails with the marinade and marinate for 2 hours.

4. Cook the marinated quails like steaks, directly over a medium heat for about 10 minutes, turning over twice.

5. Wash the rocket and coarsely tear the leaves by hand. Peel and cut the onions into rings. Clean and quarter the radishes. Combine the vegetables with the rest of the marinade on a cast-iron griddle plate and cook on all sides. Season with salt and pepper. Deglaze the griddle with the soy sauce and lemon juice.

6. Divide up the salad between four plates and arrange a quail on top or next to it.

DUCK LEG
WITH SWEETCORN

SERVES 4 AS A MAIN COURSE
READY IN: 1 HOUR 30 MINUTES
DIFFICULTY: ●●○

4 duck legs
Salt
2 ears sweetcorn
100 g/½ cup unsalted butter
2 tbsp barbecue seasoning (e.g. basic
    spice rub on page 211)

FOR THE MARINADE
6 tbsp olive oil
½ tsp wasabi paste
1 pinch mustard
1 tbsp finely chopped coriander
1 tbsp soy sauce
Juice 1½ limes
1 tbsp honey

1. Separate the legs into thighs and drumsticks at the knee joint. Bone the thighs. Lightly season the meat on both sides with salt, shape into a ball and wrap tightly in cling film. Refrigerate for 30 minutes.

2. In the meantime, mix together the ingredients for the marinade. Detach the skin from the drumsticks and peel it down like a sock. Lightly score the flesh and rub with salt and part of the marinade. Pull the skin back up over the flesh. Cut the skin around the lower part of the bone and push it upwards, so that the flesh is completely covered with skin and the bone is exposed.

3. Pull down the sweetcorn husks to expose the kernels, leaving them attached. Rub the cobs with butter and sprinkle with the barbecue seasoning. Pull up the husks again to cover the cobs.

4. Make four 8-cm/3¼-in-diameter and 4-cm/1½-in-tall rings out of aluminium foil. Press the thighs skin-side up into the rings to give their shape. Then cook with indirect heat for about 45 minutes at 180°C/350°F. Then take off the rings, turn the thighs over and cook on the skin side. Add 1–2 teaspoons of marinade to the thighs and transfer to the direct cooking side of the barbecue. Sear until the skin is brown and crispy. Cook the sweetcorn with indirect heat together with the thighs. At the same time, stand the drumsticks upright on the grid and cook for 1 hour at the same temperature.

5. Arrange a thigh and a drumstick on a plate. Use a knife to cut the sweetcorn kernels off the cobs and serve beside the duck legs. Drizzle the rest of the marinade over the meat and sweetcorn.

PULLED DUCK

BASIC RECIPE TO SERVE 6
MARINATING TIME: 4 HOURS
READY IN: 5 HOURS
DIFFICULTY: ✪✪✪

4 duck legs (each about 300 g/11 oz)
Barbecue seasoning for poultry (see
    basic spice rub on page 211, substitute
    black pepper with orange pepper and
    cayenne pepper with ground ginger)

FOR THE MARINADE
1½ tbsp salt
1 tbsp sugar

1. For the marinade, dissolve the salt and sugar in 500 ml/ generous 2 cups of water. Bone the legs and marinate for at least 4 hours, preferably overnight.

2. Take the legs out of the marinade, pat dry and rub with the barbecue seasoning.

3. Heat the barbecue to 120°C/250°F and cook the legs with indirect heat for 4–5 hours. Then take them off the barbecue, remove the skin and shred the meat. Finely chop the skin and mix with the meat. Season with barbecue seasoning or barbecue sauce.

DUCK WRAPS

SERVES 4 AS A MAIN COURSE
READY IN: 45 MINUTES
DIFFICULTY: ✪✪✪

3 tbsp sweet chilli sauce
300 g/11 oz pulled duck (see previous
    recipe)
Grated zest ½ untreated orange
3 tbsp soy sauce
½ cucumber
3 tbsp rice vinegar
1 tsp sugar
1 tsp salt
3 spring onions
4 tortillas
2 tbsp sesame seeds
2 tbsp fried onions

1. Sieve the sweet chilli sauce and set aside the solids. Heat up the pulled duck in a pan on the barbecue and season with the orange zest, chilli sauce and soy sauce.

2. Peel the cucumber, shave finely with a mandoline slicer and marinate for 30 minutes in a mixture of the rice vinegar, sugar and salt. Clean the spring onions, cut into thin rings and rinse briefly under cold running water.

3. Lay the tortillas side by side on the work surface. Make a strip of cucumber slices and spring onions along one edge of each tortilla. Lightly fold over the tortilla to cover. Then make a strip of warm pulled duck on the tortilla and roll up tightly.

4. Toast the wraps briefly on all sides over a direct heat, leaving on their meat side for 1 minute. Cut each wrap into four and serve upright on plates. Mix the solids from the sweet chilli sauce with the sesame seeds and fried onions and garnish the cut part of the wraps.

DUCK BREAST
WITH SQUASH

SERVES 4 AS A MAIN COURSE
READY IN: 45 MINUTES
DIFFICULTY: ❂ ❂ ❂

2 duck breasts, skin on
2 untreated oranges
Salt, freshly ground pepper
5 sprigs thyme, leaves plucked
2 slices bacon
1 butternut squash
1 apple
150 g/3¾ cups lamb's lettuce
1 tbsp white wine vinegar
5 tbsp pumpkin seed oil
1 pinch mustard

1. Lightly freeze the meat and then cut lengthways into strips. Trim off any excess fat. Lay the strips of each breast in a row on the work surface with the skin pointing in one direction and the ends overlapping by 2–3 cm/¾–1¼ in. Grate the zest of 1 orange. Lightly season the meat with salt, pepper and orange zest, and sprinkle with thyme.

2. Cut up the duck trimmings and bacon with a knife, as for a tartare, and season with salt and pepper. Cut off the bulbous part of the squash and set aside. Peel the neck of the squash, then use a vegetable peeler to shave off 2–3-cm/¾–1¼-in-wide strips of the flesh. Lay the strips over the meat. Roll up the strips of duck lengthways and tie with string to secure.

3. Put the rolls onto a cold plancha (smooth) griddle plate and slowly heat. Put the duck tartare on the griddle and cook until crispy. Peel the bottom bulbous part of the squash and cut out eight to twelve 3-mm/⅛-in-thick slices. Lay on the griddle with the others.

4. When the duck fat has melted, close the lid of the barbecue and cook everything for 10–15 minutes, then turn over and cook for 10 more minutes. Turn the rolls over again and cook for 5 more minutes until they reach a maximum internal temperature of 60°C/140°F.

5. Halve the second orange across the middle and peel one half. Squeeze the other half. Quarter the peeled half, cut the apple into 8–12 slices. Add the orange and apple to the griddle and cook for 5 minutes. Wash the lamb's lettuce and divide into four plates. Arrange the orange, apple and squash slices, and meat in layers over the top. Scatter with the tartare. Make a vinaigrette with the vinegar, oil, mustard, salt, pepper and 2 tablespoons of orange juice and drizzle over everything.

ASIAN-STYLE DUCK BREAST

SERVES 4 AS A MAIN COURSE
MARINATING TIME: 2 HOURS
READY IN: 45 MINUTES
DIFFICULTY: ✪✪✪

2 (200 g/7 oz) duck breasts, skin on
2 mini cucumbers
1 tsp salt
1 tsp sugar
3 tbsp sushi vinegar
100 g/½ cup unsalted butter
3 tbsp soy sauce
3–4 dashes Tabasco sauce
2 brioche burger buns, sliced in half
2 spring onions
100 ml/scant ½ cup Peking duck sauce
   (optional)
Sesame seeds, to garnish

FOR THE MARINADE
100 ml/scant ½ cup teriyaki sauce
2 star anise
3 slices untreated orange
1 pinch salt
2 tbsp sweet chilli sauce

1. Wash and pat dry the duck breasts. Trim off any excess fat. Use a sharp knife to lightly score the skin side of the breast fillets with lines about 5 mm/¼ in apart to form a cross-hatch pattern.

2. Mix together the ingredients for the marinade. Combine the meat and marinade in a ziplock bag and marinate for at least 2 hours, preferably overnight. Use a mandoline slicer to cut the cucumbers into fine shavings and marinate in a mixture of the salt, sugar and vinegar for at least 30 minutes.

3. Take the meat out of the marinade, thoroughly pat dry and lay skin-side down on a cold cast-iron griddle plate. Heat the griddle slowly on the barbecue, to allow as much fat as possible to melt under the skin. Then close the lid and cook the meat. Turn the meat over after 10–15 minutes. After another 10 minutes, turn the meat skin-side down again, and finish cooking for 5 more minutes, until the internal temperature reaches a maximum of 60°C/140°F.

4. Combine the butter, soy sauce and Tabasco sauce in a flame-proof dish and heat on the barbecue so the ingredients are mixed. Dip the cut sides of the buns in the liquid. Toast the buns on the cut sides with direct heat until sear marks develop. Cut the spring onions into thin rings.

5. Drain the cucumber shavings a little and lay over the 4 brioche halves on plates. Cut the fillets into thin slices and arrange over the cucumber. Scatter with spring onion rings. Optionally, use a squeezy bottle to drizzle with Peking duck sauce. Sprinkle with sesame seeds and serve.

CHICKEN

The flavour of chicken is generally never described as exciting, but rather as bland and boring. This prejudice is largely the result of the overwhelming preference for serving the boned and skinless breast meat of intensively reared birds. This is the equivalent of offering meat lovers dry tofu. Admittedly, the advantage of this rather neutral-tasting meat is that it gives substance to dishes without getting in the way of other flavours, whether savoury, sweet, fruity or spicy. The pectoral muscle that forms the breast originally developed to enable the bird to fly. But breeding has meant that it now only serves for meat production. In other words, the muscle has become lazy and rarely moves. The other parts of the chicken's body that are well exercised through movement are very tasty, among them the legs – drumsticks and thighs. With these different properties, every part of the chicken has its fans, and lots of delicious titbits can be prepared on the barbecue with little effort. In order to succeed, however, it is naturally important to know the right temperature and cooking times for the different parts of the bird.

YAKITORI

WINGS

LEGS

1 Head with neck and back
2 Leg
3 Wing
4 Breast

ROAMING IS KEY

The first domesticated chickens appeared in India about 8,000 years ago. Today there are some 200 breeds, which are either reared for meat or as laying hens. Depending on age and weight, distinction is made between a poussin or spring chicken, a cockerel or chicken, and a poulard. However, it isn't only a case of age and weight; diet also plays a major role and is sometimes even used as a selling point. Corn-fed chickens are well-known examples of this. There are also stewing hens and spent hens, hens that are slaughtered after they are too old to lay eggs. The chicken meat traditionally sold at supermarkets, when properly prepared, is tender and juicy, but it isn't comparable in taste to that of free-range birds. Because they are allowed to roam freely, they have a greater proportion of tastier muscle meat. Intensively reared chickens also undergo muscle development, but only in order to increase the size of the coveted breast meat. However, this sometimes has negative effects on the birds and, in the worst cases, leads to such excesses that they are barely able to bear their own weight.

Most varieties of poultry have little difference in their anatomy, and therefore the quartering process into the different cuts is similar. The breast is the muscle the bird needs to be able to fly. It accounts for about a quarter of the bird's weight and consists of a larger outer muscle, the breast fillet, and a smaller inner muscle, the mini fillet. Delicate breast meat is very popular because it has very little fat. However, care must be taken when cooking because it dries out very quickly. Leg meat in birds that don't fly or fly very rarely is much tastier than breast meat. Roaming leads to the formation of many small muscles, each separated by a thin layer of fat. The meat has a higher content in myoglobin protein, which makes it

darker. The lower part of a chicken leg is known as the drumstick.

The wings play a very minor role in terms of meat yield. They are usually considered in the same light as the giblets. Nonetheless, barbecued chicken wings are a classic.

GLAZED CHICKEN LEGS

SERVES 4 AS A MAIN COURSE
READY IN: 30 MINUTES
DIFFICULTY: ✪✪○

4 chicken legs
Salt
8 slices bacon
1 tbsp sesame seeds

FOR THE GLAZE
4 tbsp sweet chilli sauce
Grated zest 1 untreated orange
4 tbsp orange juice
3 tbsp mirin (Japanese sweet rice wine)
1 tbsp soy sauce
2 tbsp hoisin sauce
2 dashes Tabasco sauce

1. Run a knife along the bones inside the leg and remove them. Lightly season the meat with salt on both sides. Mix together the ingredients for the glaze and keep warm.

2. Cook the meat with indirect heat for about 20 minutes at 150°C/300°F. Then cook for another 15 minutes over a medium direct heat while basting repeatedly with the glaze. Also grill the bacon over a medium direct heat until crispy.

3. Serve the meat on a plate, topped with the bacon and covered with the glaze. Sprinkle over with sesame seeds.

SPICY CHICKEN WINGS

SERVES 4 AS A MAIN COURSE
MARINATING TIME: 12 HOURS
READY IN: 45 MINUTES
DIFFICULTY: ✪✪○

1 litre/4 cups chicken stock
1 tbsp Tabasco sauce
2 cloves garlic, crushed
Juice ½ lemon
2 tsp salt
1 kg/2¼ lb chicken wings
50 g/½ cup sweet paprika
1 tbsp curry powder
1 tsp freshly ground white pepper
1 tsp freshly ground coriander seeds
1 tbsp salt
200 ml/scant 1 cup basic barbecue sauce
   (see page 206)
3 tbsp cola
3 tbsp white sesame seeds

1. The previous day, mix together the chicken stock, Tabasco sauce, the garlic, lemon juice and 2 teaspoons of salt. Put the chicken wings into the marinade and cover. Marinate overnight in the refrigerator.

2. Take the wings out of the marinade and pat dry. Mix the paprika with the curry powder, pepper, coriander and salt and rub the wings with the mixture.

3. Pre-heat the barbecue to 160°C/325°F. Thread the wings onto metal skewers and cook with indirect heat for 30 minutes. Then cook over a direct heat for 5 minutes. While the wings are cooking indirectly, mix the barbecue sauce with the cola and 3–4 dashes of Tabasco sauce, and lightly warm this glaze. Baste the wings with the glaze while cooking directly during the last 5 minutes. Take the wings off the barbecue, dip in the remaining glaze, turning over, and sprinkle with sesame seeds.

STUFFED CHICKEN
BREAST FILLETS

SERVES 4 AS A MAIN COURSE
READY IN: 30 MINUTES
DIFFICULTY: ✪✪✿

4 chicken breast fillets

2 tbsp barbecue seasoning (e.g. basic spice rub on page 211)

150 g/5 oz Gorgonzola cheese

2 tbsp crème fraîche

1 tsp Worcestershire sauce

1 red chilli pepper

4 spring onions, white part only

12 slices streaky bacon

1. Halve the breast fillets across the middle. Sprinkle the cut side of the fillets with the barbecue seasoning.

2. Mix the Gorgonzola with the crème fraîche and Worcestershire sauce and spread evenly over the cut side of the fillets.

3. Cut the chilli into thin strips. Take care as the heat of the chilli remains on your fingers after cutting. Lay a spring onion and 1–2 chilli strips on four of the fillet halves. Cover each with another fillet half so that they have a uniform thickness. Wrap each breast fillet with 3 slices of bacon.

4. Cook the meat for 15–20 minutes with indirect heat until cooked through and the bacon crisps up. Just before serving, cut each roll into finger-thick slices and serve on a bamboo skewer.

CHICKEN THIGH
WITH BACON-WRAPPED RADICCHIO

SERVES 4 AS A MAIN COURSE
MARINATING TIME: 1–2 HOURS
READY IN: 30 MINUTES
DIFFICULTY: ✪✪✪

---

4 chicken thighs, boned
8 spring onions

FOR THE MARINADE
1 small clove garlic
3 tbsp teriyaki sauce
2 tbsp sweet chilli sauce
3 tbsp olive oil
Salt

FOR THE RADICCHIO
2 heads radicchio
1 clove garlic
1 small bunch thyme
Salt
6 tbsp olive oil plus extra for drizzling
1 tbsp balsamic vinegar
Freshly ground pepper
8 slices smoked and cured streaky
   bacon

1. Wash the thighs and pat dry. Use a sharp knife to pierce holes into meat. Clean and wash the spring onions and cut into 2-cm/¾-in lengths. Insert the pieces into the holes. Peel the garlic clove and crush through a garlic press. Mix the garlic with the teriyaki sauce, sweet chilli sauce, olive oil and a pinch of salt. Brush the thighs with the marinade, cover and leave to marinate for 1–2 hours.

2. Cook the thighs over a direct heat on each side for 8–10 minutes, basting regularly with the marinade. Take care that the spring onions do not come out when turning the meat over.

3. Remove the outer leaves from the heads of radicchio. Quarter the heads, keeping the leaves attached to the stalk. Peel and finely chop the garlic. Pluck the thyme leaves. Finely grind the garlic, thyme and a pinch of salt to a paste in a mortar. Mix the paste with the olive oil, balsamic vinegar and a little pepper, and drizzle the mixture over the radicchio, allowing it to run between the leaves. Set aside 1 tablespoon of the mixture.

4. Wrap each radicchio quarter with a bacon slice and secure with a cocktail stick. Leave the stalk unwrapped so that it is exposed to the full heat while cooking. The tender leaves will be protected by the bacon and acquire a delicious flavour. Drizzle each radicchio parcel with a little olive oil and cook with indirect heat at 150°C/300°F until the radicchio is tender and the bacon is nice and crispy.

TARRAGON CHICKEN
WITH SQUASH

SERVES 4 AS A MAIN COURSE
MARINATING AND SOAKING
    TIME: 9 HOURS
DRYING TIME: 12 HOURS
READY IN: 1 HOUR
DIFFICULTY: ✪✪✪

1 medium chicken
1 butternut squash
Salt
1 pinch freshly grated nutmeg

FOR THE HERB SEASONING
Juice and grated zest 1 untreated lemon
1 tbsp tarragon, finely chopped
100 g/½ cup unsalted butter, softened
1 tsp sweet paprika
1 pinch sugar
Salt, freshly ground pepper

OTHER
2 litres/8½ cups brine (2 litres/8½ cups
    water to 175 g/6 oz salt)

1. Lay the chicken breast down on the work surface. Use kitchen shears to cut along both sides of the backbones and remove. Press on the chicken to spread out and remove the breastbone. Soak the chicken for a maximum of about 8 hours in the brine. This process is known as brining. Then rinse the chicken by soaking for 1 hour in cold water, changing the water twice.

2. Take the chicken out of the water. Cut off the wing tips and any overhanging skin. Blanch the chicken in boiling water for 40 seconds and refresh in iced water for 2 minutes. Then carefully insert your hands under the skin and detach as much skin as possible from the flesh without damaging it.

3. Pat the chicken dry, place on a rack and cover with kitchen paper. Refrigerate overnight to allow the skin to dry completely.

4. The next day, remove the wishbone through the neck end of the bird. Mix together the ingredients for the seasoning. Push the seasoning under the loosened skin of the chicken and use a spoon handle to spread it out evenly. Keep the remainder of the seasoning warm. Cook the chicken, breast down, on the barbecue with indirect heat for about 30 minutes at 150°C/300°F, until the internal temperature of the breast reaches 60°C/140°F. Then raise the temperature of the barbecue to at least 200°C/400°F and continue to cook for 5–10 minutes until the skin is crispy. Baste the chicken with the seasoning as it cooks.

5. In the meantime, peel and halve the squash. Remove the seeds and fibres and cut into 2-cm/¾-in-thick slices. Season with a little salt and a pinch of nutmeg. Cook the squash with indirect heat, basting with the seasoning.

CHICKEN
FOCACCIA

SERVES 4 AS A MAIN COURSE
READY IN: 30 MINUTES
DIFFICULTY: ✪✪✪

---

4 chicken thighs, boned
Salt
1 head cos lettuce
4 slices Black Forest ham or Parma ham
8 cherry tomatoes
100 g/½ cup mayonnaise
Grated zest 1 untreated lemon
Freshly ground pepper
1 tsp sweet paprika
1 focaccia

1. Lightly salt the thighs and leave to stand for 5 minutes. Wash the lettuce, shake dry and tear the leaves into pieces.

2. Pat the thighs dry and cook over a direct heat on the barbecue at 180°C/350°F for 10–15 minutes, turning over several times. Cut the meat into slices. Place the ham slices on the barbecue warming rack to dry and crisp.

3. Halve the tomatoes (squeeze the seeds into the mayonnaise) and cut into thin strips. Stir the lemon zest into the mayonnaise and season with salt, pepper and the paprika.

4. Cut the focaccia into serving portions and spread thinly with the mayonnaise. Top with lettuce, tomato strips and chicken slices. Drizzle the meat with the remainder of the mayonnaise and garnish with crispy ham.

A robata is a type of Japanese barbecue which uses extremely hot ubame oak charcoal embers to cook small skewers of different meats and fish. For the preparation of these sort of dishes, we use the Napoleon Sizzle Zone, which can be heated to a temperature of about 900°C/1652°F.

ROBATA SKEWERS

SERVES 4 AS A MAIN COURSE
MARINATING TIME: 4 HOURS (BEEF AND CHICKEN)
READY IN: 20 MINUTES FOR EACH TYPE
DIFFICULTY: ✪✪✪

YAKITORI

4 chicken thighs, boned
1 bunch spring onions

FOR THE MARINADE

3 tbsp mirin (Japanese sweet rice wine)
2 tbsp sake
2 tbsp icing sugar
1 tsp finely chopped ginger
1 clove garlic, crushed through a garlic
   press
3 tbsp soy sauce

1. Combine the ingredients for the marinade in a pan and bring to the boil briefly in order to completely dissolve the sugar. Leave to cool. Cut the chicken into 3-cm/1¼-in squares. Put half the marinade into a bowl, mix with the meat and marinate for 4 hours.

2. Clean the spring onions and cut into 3–4-cm/1¼–1½-in lengths. Pat the meat dry with kitchen paper and thread onto skewers, alternating with the spring onions. Grill the skewers at high temperature for about 8 minutes, turning over repeatedly. Shortly before the skewers are cooked, brush with the remaining marinade and allow it to caramelise.

TERIYAKI TUNA

500 g/1¼ lb tuna
Salt
½ tsp wasabi paste
5 tbsp teriyaki sauce
2 tbsp sesame oil
2 tbsp freshly chopped coriander
2 tsp toasted white sesame seeds

1. Cut the tuna into uniform, 2–3-cm/¾–1¼-in-wide strips and season lightly with salt. Leave to stand for 10 minutes. Mix the wasabi into the teriyaki sauce.

2. Rub the fish with the sesame oil, thread onto skewers and grill at a very high temperature. Garnish by sprinkling with coriander and sesame seeds, and serve together with the wasabi-flavoured teriyaki sauce.

BEEF SKEWERS

500 g/1¼ lb sirloin

FOR THE MARINADE

4 tbsp soy sauce
2½ tbsp sesame oil
3 tbsp sake
1–2 pinch(es) five spice powder (seasoning)
Juice ½ lime
Salt

1. For the marinade, mix the soy sauce with the sesame oil, sake, five spice powder, lime juice and a pinch of salt. Cut the meat into uniform, 2–3-cm/¾–1¼-in-wide strips. Season lightly with salt and mix with the marinade. Marinate for 4 hours in the refrigerator.

2. Take the meat out of the marinade, pat dry and cook as described in the recipe for Yakitori.

FISH & SEAFOOD

Barbecued fish and seafood are no longer a rarity today, and they form a part of the essential repertoire of any discerning barbecuer. Unfortunately it can be difficult to serve up the pleasure of well-barbecued fish or seafood. Too often it is overcooked – really tender and juicy fish fillets became dry and the texture of prawns and scallops rubbery and tough. Why is that? First and foremost, it is most likely due to the fact that fish has a different protein structure to meat, which is not taken into consideration when preparing it. At barbecues, the fish and meat are typically cooked at the same time and at the same temperature for the same length of time. For a properly prepared fish, you should reduce both the cooking time and temperature in relation to a piece of meat of similar size. But I think you will find the following recipes will deliver success every time.

SARDINES

MACKEREL

SALMON

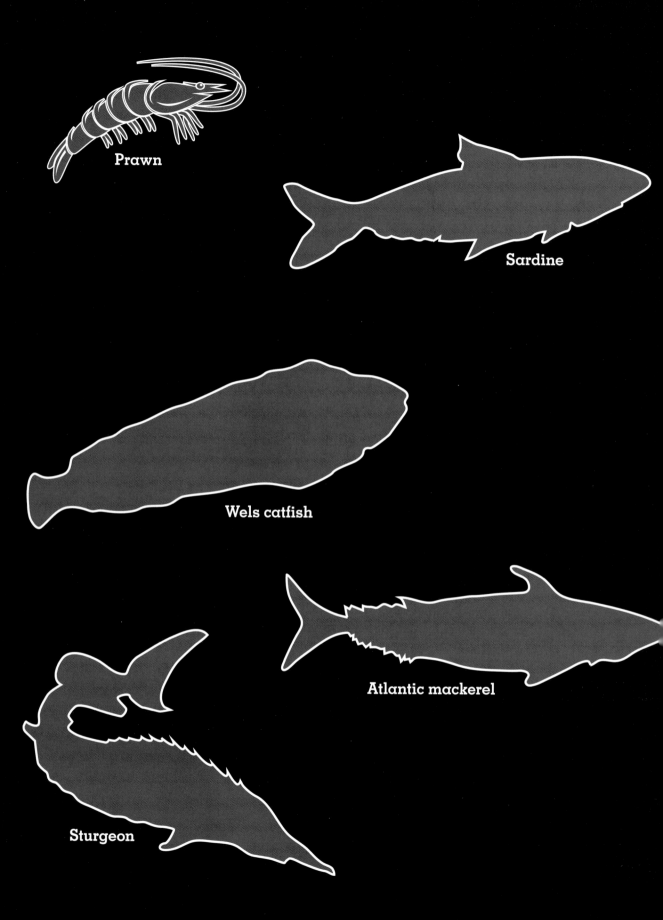

Prawn

Sardine

Wels catfish

Atlantic mackerel

Sturgeon

OUT OF THE WATER

There are a number of different ways of cooking fish and seafood on the barbecue: on a grilling plank, on a rock salt cooking block, on a stick, hung and smoked, skewered, en papillote, smoked in hay, in fillets or – for large fish like salmon and sturgeon – cooked whole.

In particular with these sensitive creatures, the timing and temperature has a crucial role if you want to end up with a juicy, tender, tasty and perfectly cooked fish on your plate. Your own experience and conversations with fellow barbecuers make the best teachers.

FLAVOUR

The subject of flavour is a very broad one. For instance, distinction is made between oily fish, such as mackerel, sardines and salmon, and lean, white-fleshed fish like cod, sole and monkfish.

Fish with a high fat content have more flavour. There are also traditional flavour combinations, such as mackerel and horseradish, salmon and cucumber, and anchovies and watercress.

The garnish always adds a certain lightness and provides a contrast. Coriander and lime are used in Asia. Salty accompaniments such as capers and ham, on the other hand, bring out the slightly sweet flavour of oily fish.

As a rule, white fish aren't as flavourful as their oily counterparts and are therefore enhanced through the use of aromatic ingredients such as dill, anise or tarragon, a sauce and a little butter, or with bacon, as in the classic Breton sole.

BUYING

Fish should also be bought according to the season. Just as tomatoes need summer sun to bring out their full range of flavours and aromas, fish shouldn't be caught out of season. For one thing, there is the very sound reason of protecting the

different species, but there is also the fact that until April, plaice is lean and full of roe. Plaice need to recover after spawning and become really tasty in late summer after a few months of feeding.

Tip: Look for special courses on barbecuing fish and seafood. You'll be given professional guidance for the proper handling and preparation of fish for barbecuing and plenty of tips and tricks to take home with you.

HERB AND FENNEL-STUFFED MACKEREL

SERVES 4 AS A MAIN COURSE
READY IN: 45 MINUTES
DIFFICULTY: ✪✪⊕

1 bunch mint
1 bunch flat-leaf parsley
2 bulbs fennel
Olive oil
4 mackerel, ready to cook
Salt, freshly ground pepper
1 lemon
2 aubergines
2 cloves garlic
2 sprigs rosemary

1. Finely chop the mint and parsley. Clean the fennel and cut off the stalk. Cut off the leaves and set aside. Use a mandoline slicer to finely shave the bulbs. Mix the fennel shavings with the herbs and 1 tablespoon of olive oil.

2. Lightly season the inside of the fish with salt and pepper, and then stuff with the herb and fennel mixture so that they bulge and can be stood on their bellies, use crumpled aluminium foil to help if necessary.

3. Position the fish on the barbecue, or alternatively, as in the photo, use a well-greased fish basket – in this case, there is no need for them to bulge so much. Cook with indirect heat for about 25 minutes at 150°C/300°F, then rub with oil and cook over a direct heat for 1 minute on each side to develop toasted flavours in their skin. Halve the lemon and cook directly on the cut sides until golden.

4. In the meantime, halve the aubergines lengthways. Peel the garlic and halve the cloves lengthways. Stud the cut sides of the aubergines with garlic halves and rosemary leaves. Drizzle each half with 2 tablespoons olive oil and cook together with indirect heat for 30 minutes. Scrape the soft aubergine flesh out of the skin and mash to a purée. Season with salt and pepper.

5. Divide the aubergine purée between four plates. Fillet the fish, lightly season with salt and drizzle with the warm lemon juice. Arrange next to the purée and garnish with fennel leaves.

MOROCCAN-STYLE SARDINES

SERVES 2 AS A MAIN COURSE
MARINATING TIME: 30 MINUTES
READY IN: 30 MINUTES
DIFFICULTY: ✪✪✪

6 sardines, ready to cook
1 lemon

FOR THE MARINADE

12 anchovy fillets in oil, drained
5 cloves garlic
2 tsp capers, drained
1 pinch each of salt, pepper, cumin,
   cayenne pepper
¼ bunch coriander, plucked
½ bunch flat-leaf parsley, plucked
A little olive oil

1. Combine all the ingredients for the marinade in a mortar and grind to a paste. Rub the sardines with a quarter of the paste and marinate for 30 minutes.

2. Pat the sardines dry and cook with indirect heat for 15–20 minutes at about 150°C/300°F, turning over twice. Then grill over a direct heat for 1 minute on each side to blister the skin. Halve the lemon and place cut-side down on the barbecue.

3. Take the fish off the barbecue and drizzle with the warm lemon juice. Serve the remaining marinade as a dip.

CATFISH FILLET
WITH FENNEL

SERVES 4 AS A MAIN COURSE
READY IN: 30 MINUTES
DIFFICULTY: ✪✪✪

2 fennel bulbs with leaves
Salt
3 tbsp olive oil
Juice 1 lemon
1 tbsp sweet chilli sauce
4 catfish fillets (200–250 g/7–9 oz each)

1. Peel off the hard outer layer of the fennel bulbs and set aside the leaves. Cut the bulbs into 1-cm-/½-in-thick slices. Season with a little salt and coat with a little olive oil. Cook the fennel slices on both sides for 5 minutes over a moderate direct heat until light sear marks appear. Then transfer to the indirect cooking side of the barbecue and cook for 20 more minutes at 120°C/250°F.

2. Finely chop the fennel leaves. Combine the lemon juice, sweet chilli sauce, chopped fennel leaves and the rest of the oil in an aluminium container and warm on the barbecue. Cook the fillets over a medium direct heat, turning over four times.

3. Arrange the fillets over the fennel slices on plates. Season fillets and fennel with salt and pepper and drizzle with the warm sauce and sprinkle with fennel leaves.

STURGEON
WITH BEETROOT SPAGHETTI

SERVES 8–10 AS A MAIN COURSE
READY IN: 1 HOUR
DIFFICULTY: ✪✪✣

1 farmed sturgeon/sterlet (1.5–2 kg/3¼–
   4½ lb), ready to cook
5 kohlrabi bulbs
500 ml/generous 2 cups beetroot juice
Salt, freshly ground pepper
3 tbsp olive oil
3 tbsp caviar

FOR THE HERB BUTTER
100 g/½ cup unsalted butter
1 tsp wasabi paste
Grated zest 1 untreated lemon
1 tsp finely chopped tarragon
Fleur de sel
Freshly ground pepper

1. For the herb butter, mix the butter with the wasabi, lemon zest and tarragon. Season with the fleur de sel and pepper, and set aside.

2. Stuff the belly of the fish with aluminium foil and lay on a grilling plank. Ideally, if you have a three-burner gas barbecue, start the middle burner and heat the barbecue to 150°C/300°F. Put the plank with the fish over the burner and cook for 30–40 minutes.

3. In the meantime, peel the kohlrabi bulbs and use a spiraliser to turn them into spaghetti. Put the kohlrabi spaghetti into a bowl, add the beetroot juice and mix until the kohlrabi turns dark red. Drain off the juice, then season with salt and pepper, and mix in the olive oil.

4. Put the kohlrabi spaghetti into an aluminium container and place on the barbecue with the fish. Put the herb butter into another aluminium container and melt on the barbecue.

5. Take the cooked fish off the barbecue. Carefully peel off the skin and fillet the fish. Put the kohlrabi on plates, arrange a piece of fish on top and drizzle with the warm melted butter. Garnish each plate with a little caviar.

ARCTIC CHAR
SANDWICH

SERVES 4 AS A MAIN COURSE
READY IN: 45 MINUTES
DIFFICULTY: ✪✪✿

4 Arctic char fillets, skin on

Salt

Vegetable oil

1 bunch dill

400 g/2 cups cream cheese

3 tbsp wholegrain Dijon mustard

2 tsp sugar beet syrup

Cayenne pepper

Juice and grated zest 1 untreated lemon

2 mini cucumbers

1 pinch sugar

2 spring onions

1 red onion

1 baguette

1. Season the flesh side of the fillets with salt and rub the skin side with oil. Lay the fillets skin-side down on a grilling plank. Put the plank directly over one of the barbecue burners on a high heat. As soon as the plank begins to smoke, lower the heat and close the lid. Cook the fish for 15 minutes with direct heat at about 150°C/300°F.

2. In the meantime, coarsely chop the dill. Mix the cream cheese with the mustard, syrup and dill. Season with salt, cayenne powder and the lemon zest.

3. Cut the cucumbers lengthways into thin slices, mix with a pinch of sugar and salt and 1 tablespoon of lemon juice, and marinate for about 10 minutes. In the meantime, clean the spring onions and cut diagonally into thin rings. Peel and finely dice the red onion and mix with the spring onions.

4. Halve the baguette lengthways across the middle and spread the cut side with seasoned cream cheese. Spread the cucumbers out over the cheese.

5. Take the fish off the barbecue and peel off the skin. If you like, toast the skin over a high heat until crispy. Arrange the fish fillets evenly over the cucumbers and cover with the onion mixture. Close the sandwich and cut into four equal portions. Optionally, garnish with the crispy skin.

PULLED
ROSEFISH

SERVES 4 AS AN INTERMEDIATE COURSE
READY IN: 30 MINUTES
DIFFICULTY: ✪✪✿

100 ml/scant ½ cup teriyaki sauce

1 tsp grated horseradish

4 rosefish fillets (about 400 g/14 oz)

2 limes

2 tomatoes

1 red onion

1 red chilli pepper

1 tbsp olive oil

Salt

1 pinch sugar

200 g/1⅓ cups sauerkraut, room
   temperature

2 spring onions, finely sliced

1. Mix the teriyaki sauce with the horseradish in a bowl. Coat the fillets with the sauce and lay on a cedar grilling plank. Place the plank with the fish on the barbecue and heat directly to a high temperature. As soon as the plank begins to smoke, lower the heat and close the lid. Cook the fish for 15 minutes with direct heat at about 150°C/300°F. Halve the limes, cook on their cut sides until soft, warming the juice and turning it sweet.

2. In the meantime, dice the tomatoes. Peel and cut the onion into julienne strips. Finely dice the chilli. Mix the tomatoes, onion and chilli in an aluminium container, squeeze the limes over the mixture and season with salt and a pinch of sugar. Mix everything well and put the bowl on the barbecue to keep warm.

3. Make a bed of sauerkraut on four plates. Shred the fish and spread over the sauerkraut. Cover with the tomato and onion salsa. Garnish with the spring onions and serve.

ITALIAN-STYLE FRENCH TOAST

SERVES 4 AS A STARTER
READY IN: 30 MINUTES
DIFFICULTY: ✪✪✿

3 eggs
200 ml/scant 1 cup milk
Salt
8 slices toasting bread
1 tomato
Freshly ground pepper
3 mozzarella balls
24 anchovy fillets in oil, drained
20 basil leaves
Balsamic vinegar

1. Beat two eggs and one egg yolk with the milk in a shallow bowl and season lightly with salt. Dip the bread slices one at a time in the mixture, turning over to soak well.

2. Finely dice the tomato and season with salt and pepper. Cut the mozzarella into thin slices.

3. Lay the cheese slices on 4 slices of bread. Cover the cheese with 6 anchovy fillets, 5 basil leaves and the diced tomato. Top with another slice of bread and press lightly.

4. Cook the sandwiches with indirect heat for about 15 minutes at 180°C/350°F until the cheese melts, pressing down on them with a spatula several times to flatten. Finally, toast the sandwiches over a direct heat for 5 more minutes, turning over twice, until golden.

5. Halve the toasted sandwiches diagonally and serve drizzled with a little balsamic vinegar.

TROUT
WITH SWISS CHARD

SERVES 4 AS AN INTERMEDIATE COURSE
READY IN: 45 MINUTES
DIFFICULTY: ❂❂○

10 thin stalks Swiss chard
4 shallots
Olive oil
1 tbsp unsalted butter
1 tbsp red wine vinegar
2 tbsp brown sugar
Salt, freshly ground pepper
2 trout, ready to cook
Grated zest 1 untreated lemon
5 sprigs thyme, plucked

1. Cut off the leaves from the chard and reserve for another use. Clean the chard stalks, washing thoroughly, and cut into 10–12-cm/4–4½-in lengths. Peel and dice the shallots.

2. Put the shallots into an aluminium container on the barbecue and sauté with 2 tablespoons of olive oil. After 5 minutes, add the chard and butter. Cover the container and simmer the chard over a low heat until tender. Season with the vinegar, sugar and salt and pepper.

3. Season the trout with salt inside and out. Season the belly cavity with lemon zest, pepper and thyme. Attach a skewer holder to the grid before heating the barbecue. Pre-heat the barbecue to 180°C/350°F.

4. Insert a skewer through each of the whole fish, close the lid and cook for 15–20 minutes until the dorsal fin can be pulled out without resistance. Take the fish off the skewers and lightly sear on both sides over a direct heat to crisp up the skin.

5. Divide the chard onto four plates. Arrange the fish over the chard. If you prefer, you can take the skin off the fish and grill separately until crisp.

Chard stalks, which are often overlooked, typically being cut up into little pieces or even discarded, are a feature of this dish.

PRAWN
MUFFINS

SERVES 4 AS A MAIN COURSE
READY IN: 25 MINUTES
DIFFICULTY: ✪✪✪

4 wholemeal English muffins

1–2 tbsp mayonnaise

12 large prawns

1 tbsp unsalted butter

Juice 1 lemon

2 tbsp celery salt

2 tbsp oregano

1 clove garlic, crushed

1 tbsp salt

½ tsp freshly ground pepper

½ banana

1 tbsp finely grated Parmesan cheese

10 basil leaves

15 watercress leaves

1. Halve the muffins across the middle, spread the halves lightly with mayonnaise and lightly toast on the barbecue until warm and soft. Put a rock salt cooking block on the barbecue and heat the barbecue to 180°C/350°F.

2. Shell and de-vein the prawns. Halve the prawns lengthways and wash.

3. Mix the butter, lemon juice, celery salt, oregano, garlic, salt and pepper in a pan on the barbecue until the butter melts. Finely dice the banana and cover the bottom half of the muffins.

4. Cook the prawns on the salt block for about 5 minutes, turning over several times. Then arrange six prawn halves on each muffin. Drizzle the seasoned butter over the prawns, sprinkle with Parmesan and garnish with basil and watercress leaves. Cover with the top halves of the muffins.

GREEN-LIPPED
MUSSELS

SERVES 4 AS A STARTER
READY IN: 10 MINUTES
DIFFICULTY: ✪ ✪ ✪

12 green-lipped (New Zealand) mussels
½ chilli pepper
1 lime
2 tbsp olive oil
1 pinch mustard
1 tsp soy sauce
1 bunch coriander

1. Cook the mussels on the barbecue with indirect heat for about 5 minutes at 150°C/300°F until they open.

2. In the meantime, finely chop the chilli and squeeze the lime. Mix the chilli and lime juice in a bowl with the oil, mustard and soy sauce. Finely chop the coriander.

3. Drizzle the mussels with a little seasoned oil, sprinkle with coriander and serve.

SCALLOP
IN A MUSHROOM

SERVES 4 AS A MAIN COURSE
READY IN: 45 MINUTES
DIFFICULTY: ✪✪✪

4 scallops
Salt
2 tbsp olive oil
1 pinch ground coriander seeds
1 pinch ground fennel seeds
100 ml/scant ½ cup chicken stock
100 g/1 cup frozen peas, thawed
50 g/¼ cup unsalted butter, melted
Freshly ground pepper
1 thin leek
2 shallots
1 tomato
1 untreated lemon
4 medium chestnut mushrooms
4 slices serrano ham
100 g/3¾ oz samphire
Pea shoots to garnish (optional)
Fleur de sel

1. Pat the scallops dry with kitchen paper. Season with salt and leave to stand for 10 minutes. Drizzle each scallop with olive oil and rub all over. Sprinkle the scallops from a height with the coriander and fennel seeds. Heat the stock. Add the peas and 1 tablespoon of butter and mash to a purée. Season with salt and pepper and keep warm. Put the remaining butter into a cast-iron frying pan and place over the side burner.

2. Remove and discard the dark green leaves and two outer layers of the leek. Slice the rest into thin rings. Peel and finely dice the shallots. Chop the tomato. Add everything to the pan. Grate the lemon zest and add. Sauté for about 5 minutes. Halve the lemon, place with the cut-side down on the grid and cook over a medium direct heat until brownish. Squeeze the lemon into the pan and keep warm.

3. Break the stems off the mushrooms and fill each cap with a tablespoon of the liquid from the pan. Cook with direct heat at about 150°C/300°F until the mushrooms absorb the liquid.

4. Hang the ham slices over three bars of the warming rack and leave to dry out at 150°C/300°F, which should take about 10 minutes. Lay the scallops seasoned-side up on the barbecue and cook for 5 minutes with indirect heat at 150°C/300°F, then cook over a direct heat for 5 more minutes, turning over after 2 minutes, until sear marks appear.

5. Take the ham off the barbecue and arrange on plates as shown in the photo. Place a mushroom in the middle of each and fill with 1 tablespoon of pea purée and 1–2 tablespoons of samphire. Arrange the scallops on top and cover with 1–2 tablespoons of the vegetables from the pan. Season with a little fleur de sel, drizzle with a little olive oil and garnish with pea shoots.

SALMON ROLL

SERVES 6 AS A MAIN COURSE
READY IN: 45 MINUTES
DIFFICULTY: ✪✪✪

1 salmon belly (approx. 500 g/1¼ lb),
   skin on with flaps
Salt
100 g/2½ cups baby spinach
1 pear
100 g/3¾ oz Gorgonzola cheese
100 g/scant ½ cup crème fraîche

1. Lightly season the fish with salt. Carefully wash the spinach and leave to drain. Use a medium grater to grate the pear and mix with the cheese and crème fraîche. Spread the mixture over the flesh side of the fish and cover with the spinach. Starting at the thicker side, followed by the thinner side, roll the salmon over the filling and tie with string to secure.

2. Cook the roll with indirect heat for about 30 minutes at 150°C/300°F. Then lay the roll over the direct heat and toast the skin until crispy. Slice the roll between the strings and serve.

HOT STONE-SMOKED SALMON FILLET

SERVES 6 AS A MAIN COURSE
READY IN: 45 MINUTES
DIFFICULTY: ✪✪✪

Top part of 1 salmon fillet, approx. 1
   kg/2¼ lb, (cut from between the head
   and middle bones), skin on
Sea salt
100 ml/scant ½ cup teriyaki sauce
Grated zest 1 untreated lemon
2 tsp seasoning mixture comprising fresh
   dill, fennel seeds, coriander seeds and
   pepper (otherwise a barbecue seasoning
   for fish or the spice rub for fish on page
   211)
1 tsp wasabi paste

ACCESSORIES
Hay

1. Heat two flat stones for 20 minutes on the barbecue. Lightly season the fish with salt. Lay a grilling plank inside the side compartment of the barbecue to protect the plastic insert. Position a small cast-iron frying pan on top of the plank and fill it with the hot stones. Cover the stones with a little hay. Lay the fish skin-side down on the hay and cover with the lid.

2. Combine the teriyaki sauce with the lemon zest, seasoning mixture and wasabi, and mix well. After 10 minutes of cooking, baste the top of the fish with this mixture. Open the lid again after 15 more minutes. Press on the edges of the fish with your finger. It is ready when the individual flakes yield.

The idea for this recipe came to me at a barbecue I was giving. The grid was already full and a guest asked me if I could cook him a piece of salmon. It was time to put my creativity to use. It was just as well I'd been wondering for some time whether the side compartment could be used for cooking... (see page 21).

VEGETABLES

Today it is impossible to imagine a barbecue without vegetables, whether as a tasty garnish or side dish or as a vegetarian main course. A lot of people prefer grilled vegetables, mushrooms or salad as a hearty meal, with fruit for dessert. Given that caterers, restaurateurs and enlightened barbecuers must assume that there will also be vegetarians present among the guests at any event, I have also come up with creative, meat-free fare to cook on the barbecue, and I'm not just referring to a couple of vegetables cooked in foil parcels. I've always had ambivalent feelings about cooked vegetables. Even as a child, I was a big fan of fresh salads. I found soft, boiled vegetables boring; leeks and cabbage would send me running from the table in winter. However, because my guests and participants in the seminars I give ask for vegetarian barbecue dishes, my curiosity was piqued. The discovery I made was that 'hot water is a vegetable's worst enemy'. So I tried preparing the vegetables I used to run away from on the barbecue. I finally discovered that it isn't hard to cook vegetables on the barbecue; you just have to be daring. You can create surprising culinary experiences by barbecuing vegetables and fruit.

AVOCADO

SQUASH

CHESTNUTS

CAULIFLOWER

SERVES 4 AS A MAIN COURSE
READY IN: 45 MINUTES
DIFFICULTY: ✪ ✪ ✪

1 cauliflower
4 cloves garlic
2 tsp sweet paprika
½ tsp freshly ground white pepper
2 tbsp unsalted butter
1 bunch parsley
100 g/1 cup shelled walnuts
4 slices Gouda cheese
1 tbsp red chilli cut into fine threads

1. Wash the cauliflower and cut off the leaves. Peel the garlic, quarter the cloves lengthways and insert the slivers between the cauliflower florets. Sprinkle the cauliflower with the paprika and pepper, and cover with small pieces of butter.

2. Wrap the cauliflower in aluminium foil and cook with indirect heat for 20 minutes at 200°C/400°F.

3. Finely chop the parsley and walnuts and mix together. Take the cauliflower off the barbecue, unwrap and discard the foil. Cover the cauliflower with the cheese slices and return to the barbecue over a direct heat and cook for 10 more minutes until the cheese melts.

4. Place the cauliflower on a serving dish and sprinkle with the walnut and parsley mixture. Garnish with chilli threads.

For meat eaters, you can cover the cauliflower with 10 slices of lardo di Colonnata or very thin slices of bacon instead of the butter.

SQUASH
QUESADILLAS

SERVES 8 AS A STARTER
READY IN: 30 MINUTES
DIFFICULTY: ✪ ✪ ✪

1 butternut squash
Salt
3 tbsp olive oil
200 g/7 oz pickled jalapeño peppers
1 red chilli pepper
4 (18-cm/7-in diameter) tortillas
200 g/2 cups grated Cheddar cheese

1. Peel and halve the squash. Remove the fibres and seeds and cut into 1-cm/½-in-thick slices. Season lightly with salt. Cook the slices with indirect heat at 160°C/325°F until they turn soft. Combine the squash with the olive oil in a bowl and crush with a fork.

2. Drain the jalapeños and cut into 5-mm/¼-in-thick rings. Split the chilli along its length, de-seed and finely dice. Mix with the jalapeño rings.

3. Spread a roughly 1-cm/½-in-thick layer of the squash over two tortillas. Sprinkle over the chilli mixture and cover evenly with the cheese. Cover with the two remaining tortillas and lightly press together.

4. Cook the quesadillas over a direct heat for 3–5 minutes on each side until the cheese melts. Take care not to let them burn.

ASIAN-STYLE
GRILLED AVOCADO

SERVES 4 AS A STARTER
READY IN: 20 MINUTES
DIFFICULTY: ⬤ ◯ ◯

2 avocados
2 tbsp olive oil
Salt, freshly ground pepper
1 tbsp wasabi paste or freshly grated
   horseradish (or from a jar)

FOR THE SAUCE

100 ml/scant ½ cup dark soy sauce
2 tbsp sugar
2 tbsp each of freshly squeezed lemon,
   lime and orange juice
1 tsp mirin (Japanese sweet rice wine)
1 tsp Worcestershire sauce
1 clove garlic, crushed

1. Mix the ingredients for the sauce together in a bowl.

2. Pre-heat the barbecue grid on the highest setting. Cut the avocados lengthways, circling the stone with the knife. Separate the halves and remove the stone. Peel them if you like.

3. Coat the flesh with the olive oil and season with salt and pepper. Lay the avocado halves cut-side down on the grid and cook over a direct heat for 3–4 minutes until dark brown stripes appear.

4. Serve the avocado halves with their cut side facing upwards and their cavities filled with sauce. Serve together with the rest of the sauce and the wasabi or horseradish.

AVOCADO
WITH CORIANDER VINAIGRETTE

SERVES 4 AS A STARTER
READY IN: 20 MINUTES
DIFFICULTY: ⬤ ◯ ◯

2 tomatoes
1 bunch coriander
Juice ½ lemon
1 tbsp olive oil
2–3 dashes Tabasco sauce
2 tsp sugar beet syrup
Salt
2 ripe avocados

1. Cut the tomatoes into 5-mm/¼-in dice and finely chop the coriander. Combine both with the lemon juice, oil, Tabasco sauce and syrup and mix well. Season with salt.

2. Halve and pit the avocados. Peel them if you like. Pre-heat the barbecue to 200°C/400°F.

3. Grill the avocados cut-side down for about 3 minutes over a direct heat. Turn over and cook with the lid closed for 3–5 more minutes. Take the avocados off the barbecue, then drizzle with the vinaigrette, and serve.

KALE AND KING OYSTER MUSHROOM BURGER

SERVES 4 AS A MAIN COURSE
READY IN: 45 MINUTES
DIFFICULTY: ✪✪✪

1 red onion

200 g/2½ cups kale

2 carrots

400 g/14 oz king oyster mushrooms

225 g/1 cup mayonnaise

120 ml/½ cup apple cider vinegar

3 tbsp sugar

1 tbsp chilli flakes

2 tbsp rapeseed oil

225 ml/scant 1 cup basic barbecue sauce
   (see page 206)

4 burger buns

ACCESSORIES

250 g/9 oz apple or cherry wood chips

1. Pre-heat the barbecue to 280°C/536°F. Peel the onion. Cut the kale and onion into very thin strips. Peel and finely dice the carrots. Clean the mushrooms.

2. Soak the wood chips in water, put into the smoking tube and place on the hottest part of the grid. If using a charcoal grill, put the wood chips directly onto the coals. Heat the wood chips in the barbecue for 15 minutes until they smoke.

3. Lay the mushrooms on the grid over a direct heat and cook for 20 minutes, turning regularly until dark. Take care they do not burn. Leave the grilled mushrooms to cool briefly and chop up with a fork.

4. In the meantime, combine the kale, carrots and onion in a large bowl. Mix the mayonnaise with the vinegar, sugar and chilli flakes, pour over the kale and mix carefully.

5. Heat the oil in a cast-iron frying pan. Add the mushrooms and barbecue sauce and sauté until the sauce is caramelised and the mushrooms are well coated. Cut the buns in half across the middle and lightly toast the cut side on the barbecue.

6. Take the buns off the barbecue, cover the bottom halves with the mushrooms and top with the kale salad. Cover with the top halves of the buns.

STIR-FRIED PADRÓN PEPPERS

SERVES 4 AS A SNACK
READY IN: 20 MINUTES
DIFFICULTY: ✪ ✪ ✪

2 tbsp sunflower oil
20 Padrón peppers
Sea salt flakes
2 tbsp grated Parmesan cheese

1. Fill the starter chimney with charcoal and light. As soon as the coals begin to glow, it is hot enough to cook with a wok.

2. Heat a wok and carefully add the oil. It is best to let it run slowly down the sides. After 10 seconds, add the peppers. Cook for 2–3 minutes until they blister, tossing in the wok every 10 seconds. Lightly season with salt and toss again. Serve on four plates sprinkled with the cheese.

Every time I had to light the charcoal barbecue using a starter chimney, I'd get annoyed that the heat produced was going to waste. So I tried cooking with a wok over the starter chimney, just to make a few snacks beforehand, which is how the idea of the stir-fried peppers came about. Of course, they can also be cooked directly on the barbecue.

FILO-WRAPPED FETA

SERVES 4 AS A SNACK
READY IN: 30 MINUTES
DIFFICULTY: ✪ ✪ ✪

20 mint leaves
100 g/2 cups chives
400 g/14 oz feta cheese
Freshly ground pepper
4 sheets filo pastry

1. Finely chop the mint and chives. Crush the cheese with a fork, lightly season with pepper and mix well with the mint and chives.

2. Cut each filo sheet into quarters. Put 1–2 tablespoons of the feta mixture on the bottom part of each filo square and roll up. Bake with indirect heat for about 20 minutes at 180°C/350°F.

CARROT HOT DOG

SERVES 4 AS A MAIN COURSE
START THE DAY BEFORE FOR FREEZING AND THAWING
READY IN: 30 MINUTES
DIFFICULTY: ●●○

4 carrots (as large as a frankfurter
    sausage, preferably in different colours)
Salt
4 hot dog buns
100 g/¾ cup coleslaw
1 red onion (optional)
2 tbsp fried onions (optional)

FOR THE MUSTARD CONDIMENT

2 apples
½ tsp grated ginger
2 tbsp sugar beet syrup
2 tbsp wholegrain mustard

1. The previous day, lightly salt the carrots, put into a freezer bag and freeze overnight. The next morning, take the carrots out of the bag and leave them to thaw at room temperature; they should become soft after an hour at room temperature.

2. Finely grate the apple and mix with the other ingredients for the mustard condiment.

3. Barbecue the carrots as you would sausages, until hot. Halve the hot dog buns lengthways across the middle and lightly toast on the barbecue.

4. Cover the bottom half of the buns with coleslaw. Place a carrot hot dog on each and spread with the mustard condiment. Optionally, add a little finely chopped red onion and fried onions. Cover with the top half of the buns and serve.

If making your own coleslaw it can be made using mayonnaise and/or yoghurt to give it more flavour and a creamier consistency than usual.

ROASTED CHESTNUTS

SERVES 8 AS A SNACK
READY IN: 30 MINUTES
DIFFICULTY: ✪ ✪ ✪

1 kg/2¼ lb chestnuts

1. Cut a cross into the skin on the rounded side of each chestnut. Put into a tumble basket, fix onto the rotisserie in front of the back burner and roast for about 30 minutes.

2. Leave the roasted chestnuts to cool a little and peel. You can eat them straight away, or use them for a purée, soup or as a garnish.

CHILLI POPCORN

SERVES 4 AS A SNACK
READY IN: 30 MINUTES
DIFFICULTY: ✪ ✪ ✪

100 g/²/₃ cup popping corn
100 g/½ cup unsalted butter
1 tsp sweet paprika
1 pinch cayenne pepper
100 g/1¼ cups freshly grated Parmesan
   cheese
Salt

1. Put the popping corn and butter into a suitably large aluminium container and cover with aluminium foil. Put the container directly over the hot grid and wait until the corn stops popping. Then take the container off the barbecue.

2. Discard any unpopped kernels and mix popcorn with the remaining ingredients.

DESSERTS

The perfect way to round off a creative barbecue menu is a delicious dessert – also prepared on the barbecue. This can be a simple grilled fruit with a fruit sauce or a creamy dip, or an innovative pastry creation on a par with something you would find in an upmarket restaurant. Desserts ranging from simple bread twists on a stick to cakes baked on the spit leave a lasting impression on all your guests, not just the children. The heat from the barbecue and the resulting caramelisation of sugars intensify the flavour of fruits, which can then be used in countless combinations including herbs such as anise, mint and rosemary, and other ingredients such as goat's cheese. The combination of hot fruit with cold ice cream is also very popular. I even find it fascinating to see how the consistency of fruits such as watermelon are transformed. If done right, it can be made to look like raw tuna. The combination of sweet and savoury elements such as banana and Comté cheese are very popular and always interesting.

FRUIT

CAKE

LOLLIPOPS

APPLE CAKE

SERVES 4 AS A DESSERT
READY IN: 30 MINUTES
DIFFICULTY: ✪ ✪ ✪

3 apples
6 eggs
150 g/1½ cups unsalted butter
1 pinch salt
Grated zest 1 untreated lemon
1 tsp ground cinnamon
Seeds from 1 vanilla pod
180 g/1⅔ cups sugar
80 g/⅔ cup pastry flour
80 g wheat starch
3 tbsp rum (optional)
Cream or ice cream, for serving

1. Peel the apples and cut off a 1-cm/½-in-thick slice from the top and bottom to allow them to fit together snugly.

2. For the cake batter, separate the eggs. Mix the butter with the salt, lemon zest, cinnamon and vanilla seeds, and finally the egg yolks. Beat the egg whites with the sugar to stiff peaks. Sift the flour together with the wheat starch. Fold the flour and starch mixture and beaten egg whites into the butter mixture, along with the rum, if using.

3. Use a knife to score the apples all over with lines about 1 cm/½ in apart. Thread the apple slices one after the other onto the rotisserie spit. Place a flame-proof dish underneath. Cook the apples over the pre-heated back burner for about 5 minutes until slightly dried. This is important as the batter will adhere to them better.

4. Brush the revolving apples with some of the batter and close the lid for about 30 seconds after each rotation. The excess batter will drip into the dish. As soon as each layer of batter turns golden, brush on the next layer. Continue until you have as many layers as you like and the apples are soft. It should resemble a traditional European spit cake.

5. Turn off the back burner and leave the cake to cool with the lid open. Carefully push the cake off the spit and cut into slices. Serve with cream or ice cream.

TRDELNÍK

SERVES 4 AS A DESSERT
READY IN: 2 HOURS 10 MINUTES
DIFFICULTY: ✪✪✪

FOR THE DOUGH

500 g/4½ cups pastry flour
30 g/⅕ cup fresh yeast
100 ml/scant ½ cup lukewarm milk
1 pinch salt
2 eggs
1 sachet vanilla sugar

FOR THE GLAZE

100 g/½ cup melted unsalted butter, plus
    butter for greasing the rolling pin
2 tbsp sugar
2 tbsp ground hazelnuts

1. Put the flour into a bowl and make a well in the middle. Crumble the yeast into the well and then add 2–3 table-spoons of milk. Mix the yeast with the milk to dissolve. Rest the yeast for 10 minutes. Add the rest of the ingredients for the dough to the bowl and knead thoroughly until smooth. Cover the dough and leave to rise for about 1 hour until it doubles in volume.

2. Knead the dough again and roll out on a floured work surface to a 1-cm/½-in thickness. Cut into 3–4-cm-/1¼–1½-in wide strips. Take the handles off a rolling pin and attach the rolling pin to the rotisserie.

3. Brush the rolling pin with melted butter and wrap the dough evenly around it. Leave the dough to prove for 30 more minutes. In the meantime, make the glaze by mixing the butter with the sugar and ground hazelnuts.

4. Position the rotisserie in the pre-heated barbecue and bake for about 15 minutes at 180°C/350°F. Brush the dough with the glaze and bake for 10–15 more minutes. To turn the trdelník dark golden and crispy, light the back burner for the last 1–2 minutes. Leave the trdelník to cool slightly and push carefully off the rolling pin.

Today trdelník is a speciality of Prague street food.

FRUIT LOLLIPOPS

SERVES 12 AS A DESSERT
READY IN: 2 HOURS 30 MINUTES
DIFFICULTY: ✪✪○

FOR THE PINEAPPLE LOLLIPOPS

400 g/14 oz tin condensed milk
200 g/7 oz Oreo biscuits, crushed
1 tbsp mint, cut into strips
1 pineapple

FOR THE MELON LOLLIPOPS

100 g/3¾ oz rice pudding
1 pinch ground cinnamon
2 Galia melons
Cereal (e.g. cornflakes)

FOR THE APPLE LOLLIPOPS

1 jar (200 g/7 oz) Nutella
4 apples
100 g/1 cup flaked almonds, lightly
   toasted

1. Boil the unopened tin of condensed milk in a saucepan for 2 hours or in a pressure cooker for 30 minutes. The tin must always be covered with water. This will caramelise the milk. Blend the rice pudding briefly and season with cinnamon. Mix the crushed biscuits with the mint. Heat the Nutella in a bain-marie.

2. Cut off the tops and bottoms of the fruits, leaving a thick middle section the height of the metal part of an apple corer. If necessary, cut the pineapple in half across the middle.

3. Use the corer to cut out cylinders from the fruits and insert a bamboo skewer into each one. Grill the lollipops over a medium direct heat until sear marks appear. Dip the lollipops into each of their corresponding coatings and sprinkle with crushed biscuits, cereal or flaked almonds.

VINEYARD PEACH WAFFLE

SERVES 4 AS A DESSERT
READY IN: 30 MINUTES
DIFFICULTY: ✪○○

4 vineyard peaches
200 g/scant 1 cup crème fraîche
2 tbsp sugar
100 ml/scant ½ cup lemon juice
3–4 sprigs mint
3 tsp lemon sherbet powder
4 waffles

1. Cook the peaches with indirect heat at 150°C/300°F until they turn soft.

2. Mix the crème fraîche well with the sugar and lemon juice. Chop the mint leaves finely. Set aside a little of the mint and mix the rest into the crème fraîche together with the sherbet powder. This will foam up after about 10 minutes.

3. Trim the waffles to the diameter of each peach. Cut the stone out of the peaches and place the fruits on the waffles. Top with the foamy crème fraîche and garnish with the rest of the mint.

WATERMELON CARPACCIO

SERVES 4 AS A DESSERT
READY IN: 1 HOUR 15 MINUTES
DIFFICULTY: ✪✪✪

1 watermelon
Grated zest 1 untreated lemon
1 tsp lemon sherbet powder

1. Cut the watermelon into twelve 10-cm/4-in x 4-cm/1½-in x 2-cm/¾-in rectangles and cook on the barbecue with indirect heat for about 45 minutes at 130°C/266°F. The watermelon will dry out a little and resemble meat. To improve the result, you can freeze the melon pieces and thaw out slowly in the refrigerator before cooking.

2. Leave to cool, slice as finely as possible and arrange slightly overlapped on a plate or serving dish. Sprinkle over with the lemon zest and sherbet powder.

FRUIT WRAP

SERVES 4 AS A DESSERT
READY IN: 45 MINUTES
DIFFICULTY: ✪✪✪

2 tbsp unsalted butter
50 g/2 cups cornflakes
4 sheets filo pastry

FOR THE FILLING
2 bananas
2 apples
200 g/7 oz fresh pineapple
5 Oreo biscuits
Flaked almonds, lightly toasted

1. Warm the butter and lightly crush the cornflakes. Halve the filo sheets and brush with the butter. Place two half-sheets on top of each other and sprinkle with the cornflakes.

2. Cut the fruit into 5-mm/¼-in dice. Crumble the biscuits and mix with the almond flakes. Lay the fruit dice in a strip along one edge of the filo sheets and add the biscuit and almond mixture, then roll up. Brush the edge of the pastry with butter and press to seal.

3. Bake the fruit wraps on a pre-heated pizza stone for 20–30 minutes at 200°C/400°F. Take them off the barbecue with care and cut into portions.

COMTÉ BANANA

SERVES 4 AS A STARTER
READY IN: 30 MINUTES
DIFFICULTY: ✪✪✪

4 ripe bananas
4 slices wholegrain toasting bread
1 tsp Espelette pepper (or chilli powder)
4 slices Comté cheese

1. Cook the unpeeled bananas for about 20 minutes with indirect heat at 200°C/400°F until the skins turn dark and the flesh becomes soft.

2. Cut open the skins and take out the flesh. Halve the bananas lengthways and lay over the bread. Season with Espelette pepper.

3. Cover the bread with the cheese and toast with indirect heat until the cheese melts.

GOAT'S CHEESE-STUFFED APRICOTS

SERVES 4 AS A SNACK
READY IN: 40 MINUTES
DIFFICULTY: ✪✪✪

4 slices bacon
8 apricots
8 small pieces soft goat's cheese

1. Cook the bacon on a cast-iron griddle plate until crispy, then drain on kitchen paper and leave to cool.

2. Cut open the apricots, remove the stone and prick the flesh several times with a fork. Replace the stone of each fruit with a piece of goat's cheese and secure the whole apricots with a bamboo skewer.

3. Place the skewered apricots on the grid and cook indirectly for about 30 minutes at 150°C/300°F. Arrange the apricots on a plate and crumble the bacon over them.

SWEET TRAMEZZINI

SERVES 4 AS A DESSERT
READY IN: 30 MINUTES
DIFFICULTY: ✪✪✪

100 g/3¾ oz dark chocolate

2 figs

3 slices tramezzini (white, crustless,
    rectangular) bread or toasting bread,
    crust removed

100 g/½ cup cream cheese

3 tbsp fig mustard

2 tbsp high-quality olive oil

1. Coarsely grate or finely chop the chocolate. Cut the figs into strips. Spread one tramezzini bread slice with half the cream cheese and sprinkle with half the chocolate. Cover with half the fig slices.

2. Spread another slice of the bread with half the fig mustard. Place the slice over the previous one with the mustard in contact with the figs. Spread the upper side of the bread with the rest of the cream cheese and cover with the rest of the chocolate and figs.

3. Spread the remaining slice of bread with the mustard and place over the previous two with the mustard in contact with the figs. Toast with indirect heat for 8 minutes on the barbecue pre-heated to 200°C/400°F, turning over once. Cut into four portions and serve.

SAUCES, DIPS
& SIDE DISHES

When barbecuing for guests, dips, fresh salads or home-made relish are essential, and they can often turn a run-of-the-mill event into a culinary highlight. Sophisticated side dishes can also distract from average-quality barbecue fare or dishes that haven't turned out quite as planned. Crudités, dips and the like have saved many a barbecue when time management has all but collapsed. Whenever I'm invited to a barbecue, I usually start up a conversation with the pitmaster by the barbecue. I secretly look around for the dips and side dishes, which are usually set up somewhere out of plain sight. I'm equally curious about the delicious recipes I read in women's magazines at the hairdresser's as I am about traditional ones handed down at home. Dishes that are often born out of the creative use of leftovers are also very good. My motto is to try as much as I can and then analyse. Why is it that delicious? Does it have the right balance of sweetness, acidity, bite, saltiness and texture? Why doesn't it taste good? Is there something missing? This information is often crucial, whether in the kitchen or at the barbecue.

RELISH

SALSA

SALAD

STUFFED LOAF

SERVES 4 AS A SIDE DISH
READY IN: 45 MINUTES
DIFFICULTY: ✪ ✪ ✪

1 round loaf farmhouse bread (500 g/1¼
   lb)
5 cloves garlic
1 ball buffalo mozzarella cheese
200 g/7 oz serrano ham, finely sliced
1 bunch rosemary
50 g/²⁄₃ cup grated Parmesan cheese
100 g/1 cup grated Cheshire cheese

1. Make five or six cuts across the top of the loaf spaced about 2 cm/¾ in apart. Cut down to 3–4 cm/1¼–1½ in from the bottom. Peel the garlic and quarter lengthwise into slivers.

2. Tear the mozzarella into walnut-sized pieces and insert into the cuts in the loaf. Do the same with the garlic and ham.

3. Pluck the rosemary leaves and sprinkle over the bread together with the Parmesan and Cheshire cheese. Bake with indirect heat for about 30 minutes at 180°C/350°F until the cheese melts.

STUFFED PIZZA

SERVES 6 AS A SIDE DISH
READY IN: 1 HOUR
DIFFICULTY: ✪ ✪ ✪

500 ml/generous 2 cups tomato passata
   (sieved tomatoes)
3 tbsp olive oil
10 basil leaves
1 sprig rosemary, plucked
4–6 sprigs thyme, plucked
Salt, freshly ground pepper
2 mozzarella balls
250 g/9 oz pizza dough
6–10 slices Parma ham
½ bunch rocket, hard stems removed

1. Put the passata and 2½ tablespoons of oil in a pan and simmer for 30 minutes until reduced by half. Finely chop the basil, rosemary and thyme, and add to the sauce. Season with salt and pepper. Remove the pan from the heat and leave to cool. Slice one mozzarella ball.

2. Roll out the dough to 5-mm/¼-inch thick and cover half with the tomato sauce. Reserve 4 tablespoons of the sauce for the topping. Cover the sauce with the mozzarella slices and fold the dough over. Use a fork or a rolling pin to carefully seal the edges of the dough.

3. Rest the dough in the refrigerator for 15 minutes, and then brush with the remaining oil.

4. Cook the pizza with indirect heat on one side at 200°C/400°F, then turn over and spread the remaining tomato sauce over the top. Tear up the second mozzarella ball and arrange over the sauce together with the ham and rocket. Cook for 15 more minutes until the cheese melts.

BASIC BARBECUE SAUCE

MAKES ABOUT 1.5 L/6¼ CUPS
READY IN: 25 MINUTES
DIFFICULTY: ✪✪✪
STORAGE: 3-4 DAYS IN FRIDGE

500 ml/generous 2 cups
  ketchup
250 ml/1 cup apple cider
  vinegar
125 ml/½ cup HP sauce

2 tbsp mustard
2 tbsp lime juice
2–3 dashes liquid smoke
2 tbsp cayenne pepper
1 tbsp sweet paprika
1 tbsp ground caraway seeds
1 tsp sugar beet syrup
700 ml/2¾ cups beef or game
  stock, depending on use

1. Mix all the
   ingredients together
   in a pan and bring
   to the boil. Simmer
   the sauce for 20
   minutes. Leave
   to cool before
   pouring into jars.

ASIAN-STYLE BARBECUE SAUCE

MAKES ABOUT 400 ML/1⅔ CUPS
READY IN: 5 MINUTES
DIFFICULTY: ✪✪✪
STORAGE: 3-4 DAYS IN FRIDGE

125 ml/½ cup hoisin sauce
3 tbsp sake
2 tbsp soy sauce
2 tbsp sugar
2 tbsp ketchup
1 tbsp rice vinegar
2 tbsp garlic paste

1. Mix all the ingredients
   together in a pan,
   bring to the boil briefly
   and pour into jars.

YAKITORI SAUCE

MAKES ABOUT 500 ML/GENEROUS 2
  CUPS
READY IN: 20 MINUTES
DIFFICULTY: ✪✪✪
STORAGE: 3-4 DAYS IN FRIDGE

1 red onion
200 ml/scant 1 cup soy sauce
200 g/1 cup demerara sugar
3 tbsp mirin (Japanese sweet
  rice wine)
Grated zest 1 untreated lemon
3 tbsp chicken stock

1. Peel the onion and cut
   into thin rings. Combine
   the onion with the other
   ingredients in a pan
   and bring to the boil.
   Simmer for about 10
   minutes. Strain the sauce
   and pour into jars.

POMEGRANATE GUACAMOLE

SERVES 8 AS A DIP
READY IN: 15 MINUTES
DIFFICULTY: ⊘⊘

3 avocados
Juice and grated zest 1 untreated
   lime
1 tsp finely chopped chilli pepper
Salt
1 pomegranate
1 sprig mint, leaves finely
   chopped

1. Halve the avocados lengthways and remove the stone. Scoop the flesh out into a bowl. Finely mash four avocado halves with a fork and add the lime zest and a little juice. Season with the chilli and salt.

2. Halve the pomegranate and scoop out the seeds. Dice the two remaining avocado halves and carefully mix with the mint, pomegranate seeds, a little lime juice and salt.

3. Fold the pomegranate seeds and avocado dice into the mashed avocados and serve.

GUACAMOLE WITH CUCUMBER

SERVES 4 AS A DIP
READY IN: 5 MINUTES
DIFFICULTY: ⊘⊘

cucumber
avocado
Salt
Juice ½ lemon
2 dashes Tabasco sauce

1. Peel and halve the cucumber lengthways. Scrape out and discard the soft flesh and seeds. Halve the avocado lengthways and remove the stone. Scoop out the flesh into a bowl.

2. Cut the cucumber into small pieces and add to the avocado. Season with a pinch of salt, the lemon juice and Tabasco sauce, then mash.

PONZU GUACAMOLE

SERVES 6 AS A DIP
READY IN: 15 MINUTES
DIFFICULTY: ⊘⊘

2 avocados
1 red onion
2 tbsp ponzu sauce
1 pinch wasabi paste

1. Peel and halve the avocados lengthways and remove the stones. Lay cut-side down on the hot grid until sear marks appear. Peel and cut the onion into julienne strips.

2. Finely dice the avocado flesh and mix with the onions, ponzu sauce and wasabi.

BUTTER INJECTION FOR CHICKEN

MAKES ENOUGH FOR 3 KG/6½
    LB MEAT
READY IN: 15 MINUTES
DIFFICULTY: ★★

1 chilli pepper
250 ml/1 cup chicken stock
4 tbsp unsalted butter
2 tbsp lemon juice
Salt

1. Cut open the chilli and de-seed.
   Combine the other ingredients in a
   pan and heat, without bringing to
   the boil. Add the chilli.

2. Leave the liquid to cool to
   room temperature so that the
   butter remains liquid. Remove
   and discard the chilli and fill a
   marinade injector with the liquid.

INJECTION FOR PULLED PORK

MAKES ENOUGH FOR 3 KG/6½ LB MEAT
READY IN: 20 MINUTES
DIFFICULTY: ★★

500 ml/generous 2 cups apple
    juice
1 tbsp salt
10 slices bacon, finely diced
2 tbsp brown sugar
2 tbsp light soy sauce
2 tbsp Worcestershire sauce
1 tbsp chilli sauce

1. Combine all the ingredients
   in a pan and bring to the
   boil.

2. Remove the pan from the
   heat and leave to cool.
   Strain and fill a marinade
   injector with the liquid.

INJECTION FOR BEEF

MAKES ENOUGH FOR 10 KG/20 LB
    MEAT
READY IN: 10 MINUTES
DIFFICULTY: ★★

2 tbsp salt
2 tbsp rice vinegar
1 tbsp sugar
2 tbsp soy sauce
700 ml/2¾ cups beef stock
1 tbsp chilli sauce (preferably
    sriracha sauce)

1. Combine all the
   ingredients in a
   bowl and mix until
   the sugar and salt
   dissolve. Fill a
   marinade injector
   with the liquid.

2. Store leftover
   liquid in a jar in
   the fridge for up
   to a week.

BASIC MARINADE

MAKES ENOUGH FOR
1 KG/2¼ LB MEAT
READY IN: 10 MINUTES
DIFFICULTY: ✪✪

1 untreated lemon
1 red chilli pepper
2 cloves garlic
½ tsp salt
1 tbsp soy sauce
1 tsp finely chopped parsley
1 tsp finely chopped thyme
125 ml/½ cup olive oil

1. Grate the lemon zest and set aside, then squeeze the lemon. Finely dice the chilli. Peel and chop the garlic.

2. Combine the salt with the chilli, soy sauce and lemon juice in a bowl and mix well. Add the lemon zest, garlic, parsley and thyme. Finally, mix in the olive oil.

MARINADE FOR GAME

MAKES ENOUGH FOR 5 KG/11
LB MEAT
READY IN: 20 MINUTES
DIFFICULTY: ✪✪✪

700 ml/2¾ cups red wine
2 tbsp gin
125 ml/½ cup balsamic vinegar
125 ml/½ cup olive oil
1 red onion, finely diced
1 carrot, finely chopped
1 stick of celery, finely chopped
2 cloves garlic, crushed

2 bay leaves
2 cloves
1 tsp dried thyme
3 tbsp finely chopped flat-leaf parsley
10 black peppercorns
10 juniper berries

1. Combine all the ingredients in a pan and briefly bring to the boil. Leave to cool before use.

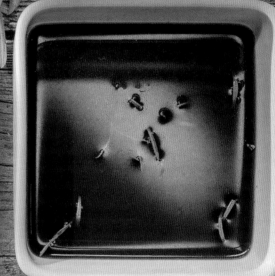

TERIYAKI MARINADE

MAKES ENOUGH FOR 500 G/1¼ LB MEAT
READY IN: 5 MINUTES
DIFFICULTY: ✪✪

3 spring onions
125 ml/½ cup soy sauce
125 ml/½ cup mirin
4 tbsp honey
4 tbsp sesame oil
1 tsp ginger paste
2 tsp garlic paste

1. Finely dice the white part of the spring onions. Cut the green leaves into thin rings.

2. Carefully mix the soy sauce with the mirin and honey in a bowl. Mix in the remaining ingredients.

TOMATO AND CORIANDER RELIS

SERVES 4
READY IN: 15 MINUTES
DIFFICULTY: ●●

3 tomatoes (preferably oxheart
   tomatoes)
1 small red onion
1 red chilli pepper
½ tsp garlic paste
2 tbsp finely chopped coriander
Juice 1 lime
Salt

1. Halve and de-seed the
   tomatoes. Peel the onion.
   Halve the chilli lengthways
   and de-seed.

2. Finely dice the tomatoes and
   onion, and finely chop the
   chilli. Combine everything
   in a bowl and mix in the
   remaining ingredients.
   Season with salt.

WATERMELON RELISH

SERVES 4
READY IN: 15 MINUTES
DIFFICULTY: ●●

1 watermelon
1 cucumber
1 red onion
2 chilli peppers
3 tbsp demerara sugar
Juice 2 limes
1 tsp ginger paste
1 tbsp finely chopped mint

1. Halve the watermelon and
   scoop out the soft flesh
   into a bowl and mash to a
   purée.

2. Peel the cucumber and
   discard the seeds. Finely
   dice the flesh. Peel and
   finely dice the onion. Halve
   the chillies lengthways,
   de-seed and finely dice.

3. Put all the ingredients
   together watermelon
   purée, and mix.

BASIC SPICE RUB

MAKES ENOUGH FOR 2 KG/4½ LB MEAT
READY IN: 10 MINUTES
DIFFICULTY: ✪✪

4 tbsp coarse salt
4 tbsp dark muscovado sugar
2 tbsp sweet paprika
3 tbsp freshly ground pepper
1 tbsp garlic powder
½ tsp cayenne pepper
½ tsp celery seeds

1. Mix all the ingredients well in a mortar and fill a storage jar with a tight seal.

SPICE RUB FOR FISH

MAKES ENOUGH FOR 5 KG/11 LB FISH
READY IN: 15 MINUTES
DIFFICULTY: ✪✪

150 g/¾ cup demerara sugar
100 g/½ cup salt
2 tbsp freshly ground pepper
1 tbsp dried dill
1 tsp coriander seeds
1 tsp fennel seeds

1. Mix all the ingredients well in a mortar and fill a storage jar with a tight seal.

ONION RELISH

SERVES 4
READY IN: 15 MINUTES
DIFFICULTY: ✪✪

1 Spanish onion
1 tomato
5 tbsp white wine vinegar
1 tsp salt
½ tsp cayenne pepper
2 tbsp olive oil
1 tbsp finely chopped coriander

1. Peel the onion. Finely dice the onion and tomato and mix with the remaining ingredients.

SPICE RUB FOR PORK

MAKES ENOUGH FOR 2 KG/4½ LB MEAT
READY IN: 15 MINUTES
DIFFICULTY: ✪✪

4½ tbsp coarse salt
2 tbsp freshly ground white pepper
2 tbsp freshly ground black pepper
2 tbsp dried parsley
1 tbsp cumin
1 tbsp oregano
1 tbsp garlic powder

1. Mix all the ingredients well in a mortar and store in a jar with a tight seal.

PEBRE (CHILEAN SALSA)

SERVES 4 AS A DIP
READY IN: 15 MINUTES
DIFFICULTY: ✪✪✪

2 bunches spring onions
2 beef tomatoes
1 red chilli pepper
1 bunch coriander
3 tbsp olive oil
Fine sea salt

1. Cut the spring onions into thin rings. Cut the tops off the tomatoes and de-seed, then finely dice. Slit open the chilli along its length, de-seed and finely dice. Finely chop the coriander.

2. Combine the diced and chopped ingredients with the oil in a bowl and mix well. Season with salt.

WALNUT AND GARLIC DIP

SERVES 4 AS A DIP
READY IN: 5 MINUTES
DIFFICULTY: ✪✪✪

4 cloves garlic
200 g/2 cups shelled walnuts
150 ml/⅔ cup olive oil
Salt

1. Peel the garlic. Crush the walnuts and garlic cloves in a mortar to a paste, gradually working in the olive oil. Season the dip with salt.

CARROT AND PEANUT DIP

SERVES 4 AS A DIP
READY IN: 15 MINUTES
DIFFICULTY: ✪○○

4 carrots
75 g/¾ cup roasted and salted
   peanuts, chopped
1 tbsp balsamic vinegar
2 tbsp peanut oil
4 drops sesame oil

1. Coarsely grate the carrots into a bowl
    and mix with the remaining ingredients.

CHILLI AND CORIANDER DIP

SERVES 4 AS A DIP
READY IN: 10 MINUTES
DIFFICULTY: ✪○○

1 bunch coriander
4 green chilli peppers
1 cucumber
Juice ½ lemon
1 tbsp sugar beet syrup

1. Chop the coriander finely. Split the chillies along their length,
    de-seed and dice finely. Halve the cucumber lengthways, scrape
    out and discard the soft flesh and seeds and dice the flesh finely.

2. Mix the lemon juice with the syrup in a bowl and mix well. Mix in
    the chillies and cucumber, followed by the coriander. Season the
    dip with salt.

MOOLI SALAD

SERVES 4 AS A SIDE DISH
READY IN: 15 MINUTES
DIFFICULTY: ✪

1 mooli
1 red chilli pepper
1 tbsp salt
4 tbsp sugar
4 tbsp rice vinegar

1. Peel and thinly slice the mooli. Stack the slices and cut into fine strips. Split the chilli along its length, de-seed and finely dice.

2. Combine the chilli, salt, sugar and vinegar with the mooli in a bowl and mix well. Leqve to stand for 30 minutes before serving.

SPRING ONION SALAD

SERVES 4 AS A SIDE DISH
READY IN: 15 MINUTES
DIFFICULTY: ✪ ✪ ✪

10 spring onions
1 red chilli pepper
4 tbsp soy sauce
1 tbsp sesame seeds
1 tbsp sesame oil

1. Clean the spring onions. Cut each onion first into three equal lengths, then cut into fine strips. Put into a bowl. Finely dice the chilli.

2. Mix the soy sauce, chilli, sesame seeds and sesame oil well and pour over the spring onion strips.

FOUR-ONION SALAD

SERVES 4 AS A SIDE DISH
READY IN: 15 MINUTES
DIFFICULTY: ✪

1 Spanish onion
2 red onions
1 white onion
4 spring onions
1 tbsp finely chopped
   flat-leaf parsley
2 tbsp white wine vinegar

3 tbsp olive oil
2 tbsp medium-strength
   mustard
1 tbsp sugar beet syrup
Salt, freshly ground
   pepper

1. Peel and finely slice the onions. Cut the spring onions into fine rings.

2. Mix the remaining ingredients together for the dressing. Mix the dressing into the onions. Leave to stand for 30 minutes before serving.

SWEETHEART CABBAGE SALAD

SERVES 4 AS A SIDE DISH
READY IN: 15 MINUTES
DIFFICULTY: ✪

1 sweetheart cabbage
2 tsp salt
1 apple
Juice 1 lime
2 tbsp sweet chilli sauce
1½ tbsp sherry
1 tsp wholegrain mustard
2 tbsp olive oil

1. Use a mandoline slicer to shave the cabbage finely. Season with salt and knead well into the cabbage. Core the apple and cut into julienne strips. Carefully mix the apple together with the cabbage.

2. Combine the remaining ingredients in a bowl and mix well. Add to the apple and cabbage and mix well.

MENU SUGGESTIONS

CHRISTMAS MENU WITH GAME

Starter:
Tagliata with onglet
   steak
Page 54

Intermediate course/
side dish: Sweetheart
cabbage salad
Page 215

Main course:
Leg of roe venison with
rosemary-studded apples
Page 112

Dessert:
Watermelon carpaccio
Page 196

CHRISTMAS MENU WITH DUCK

Starter:
Trout with Swiss chard
Page 162

Main course:
Asian-style duck breast
Page 129

Dessert:
Trdelník
Page 192

MEDITERRANEAN MENU

Starter:
Italian-style French toast
Page 160

Intermediate course/
snack: Stir-fried
Padrón peppers
Page 183

Main course:
Leg of rabbit with
sweet potato
Page 120

Dessert:
Comté banana
Page 198

HALLOWEEN PARTY MENU

Starter:
Squash quesadillas
Page 177

Snack:
Roasted chestnuts
Page 187

Main course:
Stuffed hokkaido
squash
Page 106

Dessert:
Apple cake
Page 191

ASIAN-STYLE MENU

Starter:
Asian-style grilled
avocado
Page 178

Main course:
Robata skewers
Page 145

Dessert:
Watermelon carpaccio
Page 196

BURGER MENU

Starter:
Mini burgers of your
choice
Pages 65–67

Main course 1:
Rummel burger 2.0
Page 56

Main course 2:
Ramen burger
Page 59

Dessert:
Fruit lollipops or
Vineyard peach waffle
Page 195

INDEX

ACKNOWLEDGEMENTS

The most enjoyable part of writing a book is expressing thanks to all the people who contributed to making it a reality.

NAPOLEON GOURMET GRILLS (www.napoleongrills.de)
During the course of my career I have had the opportunity to cook on barbecues made by several manufacturers. I have been using Napoleon products for some years now, and I am very happy with them. The company produces high-quality, innovative and functional products.

Bos Food
Extremely competent service, friendly staff and first-rate products, and always up to date. Ralf Bos and his team – especially the crew from the production kitchen led by Achim Eisenberger – have supported and advised me ever since I began my barbecuing career.

Fleischerei Fessel
The Fessels are a traditional and innovative business with charm. Metzger Fessel is the butcher I trust. As they say: 'If you become friends with your butcher, you will also have good meat!'

SK Leasing
A friendship that began at school has, through creative cooperation with Kathrin and Stephan, turned into a successful team, which has been a great support for me for years.

Thanks also go to the team at **Fotografen Dirk Tacke**. We spent days working hard on the set, but it was a lot of fun and the pictures turned out great.

A big thank you to my family, who over the last few years have always been a support to me in both word and deed.

Thank you **Lotti and Helmut**

Published in 2020 by
Grub Street
4 Rainham Close
London
SW11 6SS

Email: food@grubstreet.co.uk
Web: www.grubstreet.co.uk
Twitter: @grub_street
Facebook: Grub Street Publishing

Copyright this English language edition © Grub Street 2020

Copyright © 2016 Christian Verlag GmbH, Munich
Originally published in German as *Grillen Grillsaison ist jeden tag*
Layout: Silke Schüler
Texts and recipes: Andreas Rummel
Photography and styling: Dirk Tacke

Food styling: Brigitte Tacke
Photography assistance: Clarissa Nill

A CIP catalogue record for this book is available from the British Library.

ISBN 978-1-911621-35-5

Printed and bound in India